A Sparrow Among the Bluebirds

By Wayne Barham

Wayne Barham • Springfield, South Dakota

Copyright © 2004
Wayne Barham

ALL RIGHTS RESERVED
This work may not be used in any form, or reproduced by any means, in whole or in part, without written permission from the publisher.

Library of Congress Control Number: 2004108478

ISBN: 1-57579-290-7

First printing 2004

Printed in the United States of America
PINE HILL PRESS
4000 West 57th Street
Sioux Falls, SD 57106

Dedication

To my family,

To my students,

To my comrades that I served with
in K Company, Ninth Marines, WWII.

It took me 30 years to write this book. I hope you enjoy it.

Love & Semper Fi,

Wayne Barham

Table of Contents

PART ONE
The Little Red Wagon 1

PART TWO
World War II..19

PART THREE
Educational Potpourri...39

PART FOUR
Two Different Worlds 49

PART FIVE
Counseling Experience 55

PART SIX
1967-1983 76

PART SEVEN
Dogs 122

Acknowledgments

A grateful thank you to Mary Hurd who put my pen and ink scribblings into a manuscript.

Part One

The Little Red Wagon

The economy of the United States wasn't exactly booming in 1935. I was eleven years old, and my dad was working for twelve dollars a week in our hometown of Champaign, Illinois. Double-dip ice cream cones, pop and hamburgers sold for a nickel. The Saturday afternoon cowboy movies featuring Ken Maynard, Hoot Gibson, and Tom Tyler cost a dime. My problem was that I never had a dime.

On our block it was said that the farther you went, the tougher the neighborhood got...and we lived in the last house. The Illinois Central Railroad tracks ran right past my bedroom window. Our house trembled when the steam locomotives rumbled past, and the dishes shook on the kitchen table.

Directly opposite our house on the other side of the railroad tracks sprawled an ugly junkyard. The owner, known only as Sam, was short and bald. He wore the first horn-rimmed glasses I had ever seen. They fascinated me. I never really noticed what his face looked like. I could only stare at him...the man with the big, horn-rimmed glasses.

One evening after school, I was hanging around the junkyard staring at Sam's glasses and killing time. Trucks and cars were coming and going. The drivers unloaded assorted junk and piled it on scales to be weighed. Sam would peer intently at the scales and then reach into his front pocket to produce a handful of coins and a roll of bills. I watched as he paid his customers. I needed money to attend the Saturday afternoon cowboy movies. Here was my answer! I could collect junk in my neighborhood and sell it to Sam. Whose neighborhood had more junk in it than mine?

I arose early on Saturday morning and ventured forth, pulling my little red wagon behind me. I walked up and down alleys and knocked on doors, asking for old newspapers, magazines, bottles, rags, copper wire, and iron. I thought of myself as a businessman. The neighborhood people called me "the little scavenger."

When the wagon was full, I hustled over to the junkyard to have the loot weighed. I piled it on the scales and watched breathlessly as Sam reached into his front pocket for my money.

"Here, kid," he mumbled as he held out a dime. That damned crook. I had expected much more. And yet it was the price of a ticket to the cowboy show. I snatched the dime from his hand and ran downtown to the theater. After all, Tom Mix and his wonder horse, Tony, would soon be flashing across the screen.

This same routine continued for several weeks. Each Saturday morning I was paid ten cents for my wagonload of junk. No matter how much junk I brought to Sam, my reward was always the same, ten cents. I began to lose my interest and drive as a businessman. Each successive Saturday morning found me loading less junk into my wagon.

It was then that I turned to a life of crime. A high, wooden fence surrounded Sam's junkyard. It must have stood eight feet tall. The boards were rough and unpainted. The yard inside the fence was filled to capacity with the normal clutter you would expect of any junkyard. Sam and his workers were forced to pile overflow scrap iron outside the fence on the ground. I decided to steal Sam's own iron and sell it back to him. It would serve the old crook right.

The following Saturday morning, I picked up my little red wagon and carried it quietly across the tracks. I tiptoed up to the big board fence and very gently eased the wagon to the ground. Then I stealthily began to fill it with iron. My heart was pounding in my skull, and I cast many furtive glances in all directions.

I was absolutely certain that if I were caught, the judge would sentence me to the penitentiary for twenty years. At least! A quick bit of mental arithmetic showed that I would be an old man of thirty-one before I would be released from jail. I was sweating like mad and nearly chickened out. And then I had a vision of Ken Maynard riding across the screen on his white horse, Tarzan. Having defeated my conscience, I began whistling nonchalantly as I pulled my loaded wagon along the fence to the big, open door. The wagon was guided onto the scale. Sam glanced at it quickly and said, "Here, kid," as he flipped me a dime. I smiled inwardly. My revenge was complete. I thought how much easier this was than playing the role of neighborhood scavenger.

My life of crime continued for another year. I was much more mature at the age of twelve. My diabolical mind hit upon a scheme to produce more money with half the labor involved. I would build sideboards on my wagon that would double its load capacity. This would enable me to receive twenty cents per load. I would have to go to the junkyard only every other Saturday. The cold business world had spawned a shrewd, calculating twelve-year-old. I was my own efficiency expert. Perhaps the words "expertise" and "consultant" hadn't been coined as yet in 1936, but I was moving in that direction.

When the sideboards had been crudely installed, I brazenly approached the big wooden fence and piled twice as much iron into my wagon. Around, the corner, through the gate, and onto the scale. Sam never batted an eye. "Here, kid," he said as he tossed me my usual dime. That really did it. This cheap old crook was cheating me, but what could I say? He was holding the best cards, and it was the only game in town. After the matinee cowboy movie, I went home and ripped the sideboards off my wagon. A pox on Sam, and I hoped the rats would carry off his lunch.

I was obsessed with the subjective reality that I was being had by a cunning, old crook, but I resigned myself to Sam's weekly ten-cent fleecings. He just plain beat me. My heart wasn't in it anymore. I gradually loaded less and less of Sam's iron into my wagon.

The Great Depression struck just as I entered elementary school. I was off to a poor start, because I was denied kindergarten. I had to play catch-up. My parents couldn't afford to pay the tuition fee, so only the rich kids went to kindergarten.

About halfway through the school year our teacher divided us into three groups. It was obvious that the smart kids were bluebirds, the robins were the average kids, and we dumb kids were the sparrows. We were herded into our groups for the various activities.

There were six or seven grade schools in town. Miss Farland and Miss Dose were the music teachers, and they visited all the schools. One day they announced that we were starting a rhythm band. They produced two big boxes of instruments. They began to pass out wood blocks, triangles, cymbals, tambourines, and a myriad of sticks. Teachers have a way, a gift, of looking at students and determining whether they are smart or dumb. How do they do this? They took one look at me and surmised that I must have missed kindergarten. Therefore, I was handed a pair of sticks. The stick section constituted about 70% of the band. As Miss Dose played the piano, we little percussionists struck our instruments. Our section sounded like twenty angry crickets all marching to a different beat.

The next year, I asked my new teacher if I could play the triangle. She asked what had I played last year? The sticks. "Well, then, you should be a stick man again."

The following year was more of the same. I wanted so much to play that triangle. The sound reminded me of the wind chimes on my grandma's porch. But my teacher said, "Evidently, you don't have any musical talent, so just try to be the very best in the stick section. Nothing wrong with that."

During this period of time in the Thirties, the big event of the year was the "free show" at Christmastime for all elementary school kids. It was sponsored by the biggest theater in town. It could seat 1,600 kids. Think about it. All these unsupervised little urchins and never a problem. One uniformed usher with a flashlight easily controlled the well-behaved horde. Each kid was asked to bring something for the poor. Sort of a food pantry idea. I always took a jar of my mother's home-canned fruit or vegetables. I asked myself each year, "Who gets all this stuff?" I didn't know anyone poorer than we were.

We are talking about a town of 25,000 people, but there were so few cars, we played ball in the streets. Can't remember playing with a new ball. The cover would come apart, so we stuffed the ball with sand, sawdust, or rags and sewed the cover together again. Old Mr. Lee had a shoe repair shop, and sometimes he was kind enough to use his special tools to help us as we watched.

Then a new kid named Edward moved into the neighborhood. We soon discovered that he had a new football, new sled, and new baseball bat (ours was split and nailed and taped together). Edward even had a brand new baseball glove that smelled really swell.

Edward's parents weren't rich, but they had a friend, Mr. Vogel, who was a traveling salesman. He came through town four or five times each year and stayed overnight with them. He always had a gift for Edward.

One day Edward said, "Mr. Vogel is taking me to a movie today, and he told me I could bring a friend. Would you like to come along?" Dumb question. So the three of us are soon in the lobby of the theater. Mr. Vogel buys us popcorn and suggests a candy bar, too. I can't believe this...a free show, popcorn, and a box of Milk Duds. It doesn't get any better than this. We go into the theater. Mr. Vogel maneuvers Edward into a row first, then he is next, and I am last. We take off our coats and hold them on our laps. The lights dim. I feel a hand on my knee. No problem. What a nice friendly gesture. Then the hand begins to move up my thigh. Now this is a problem. I have popcorn in one hand and a box of Milk Duds in the other. I need another hand. I manage to push the hand away. Moments later, the hand is back. This time more insistent. I look over at Edward. In the darkness I can still see that Mr. Vogel's other hand is busy under Edward's jacket. Edward is intent upon watching the movie as he munches popcorn. I push the hand away again. As young as I am, I realize the destination of this hand is supposed to be my crotch. I thwarted a few more attempts. The hand gave up. Mr. Vogel continued to visit Edward's home, but I was never again invited for a free movie. Big deal! I already had a baseball mitt.

I first discovered a great difference in boys and girls when Mildred moved to our town from Chicago. She smiled and asked me my name. I couldn't answer. Her blue eyes held me speechless. I vowed to take her to a movie. How do I get the money? I worked my butt off, that's how. I mowed giant lawns for 25 cents. One old lady complained that I didn't get down on my knees and trim the edges of the sidewalks. I spaded gardens by hand. I shot and dressed cottontail rabbits. Sold them ready for the pan for twenty cents. Can you picture an eleven-year-old boy walking through a city, headed for the country, carrying a .22 rifle or a 20-gauge shotgun? And right past the posh private country club golf course. Buying rifle and shotgun shells was easy. I could go into any store that sold ammo, tell them what I wanted, and I didn't have to fill out a form asking for my name, age, and address. There were no school shootings in the Thirties. Of course, this was also before Xerox, credit cards, TV, air conditioners, and panty hose. "Made in Japan" meant junk.

This was my first love. First date. Bus fare, movie, popcorn. I was afraid to go up to her house and ring the bell. I shouted her name from the sidewalk and hid behind a tree. I lucked out. Mildred was waiting for me. And what did Mildred have to offer? All she had to do was smile, look deep into my soul with those eyes and perhaps touch my hand. Women have such power. Men have made fools of themselves over women for eons. Powerful industrialists, leaders of great nations, famous and infamous men. And some day Mildred will add cleavage to her arsenal of weapons. Cleavage is what men want. But it is like looking at the sun. You don't stare. You just peek and look away.

Forty years after Marilyn Monroe died, her name is still magical. Norma Jean Baker became a world-famous sex object. That's the way it has always been. The ladies may deplore it, but if women weren't sex objects, men would not do the insane things they do to win their hearts...and become their slaves. Women have always been more powerful than kings.

The word got out that Mildred could run really fast. I was the fastest boy in our class. The guys said I should race her. They called me chicken and goaded me with other remarks. I couldn't refuse. The male ego. Mildred agreed to a race during recess. We agreed to run perhaps 40 or 50 yards from the Bone Ditch (the stinky stream) to the corner past the swings. To my dismay, the entire class turned out to watch. We lined up. I crouched slightly, looked to my left, and was shocked to see Mildred hike up her skirt and get down in a four-point sprinter's stance. (Girls didn't wear pants to school.) I realized I could be in a heap of trouble here. All she lacked was a set of starting blocks. I beat her by a stride. I wonder if she let me win? I'll never know. Women are devious.

Our school janitor (excuse me, custodian) was a nice old guy. Mr. Potts had a beautiful gold pocket watch on a huge chain. We didn't have an electronic school bell for recess. Different grades had their own times for the playground. Mr. Potts would appear from the basement, watch in hand, and ring a handheld bell to summon us back into the building. I decided it would be interesting to steal the bell and hide it in some bushes. It was chaos. Kids were herded into one door, and they went right out another. Classes overlapped. I was careful not to be caught when I returned the bell. The next day, I asked permission to go to the bathroom. I went to the basement where the bathrooms were located. As I walked past the open door to the boiler room where Mr. Potts shoveled coal, I saw him hanging from a beam...still twisting slowly. I ran back upstairs and whispered to my teacher what I had seen. She didn't believe me but followed me downstairs. I can still hear her gasp. Surely there was no connection between the bell episode and his suicide. Yet, I live with the guilt.

Once in awhile a woman appeared to teach us handwriting skills. She was probably the forerunner of later visiting or traveling teachers. She told us that this was the Palmer Method of writing. She always demonstrated how to hold the pen and then how to write with it. She hovered over me and was not pleased. She produced a thumbtack and stuck it in my elbow to illustrate how the holding of the pen, the wrist, and the forearm should all be part of one fluid motion. Behavior modification hadn't arrived yet.

At Easter time, the hatchery filled its large front window with cute tiny baby chickens. They were dyed pastel shades of yellow, blue, and pink. My parents had a chicken pen (in town, mind you) where they usually kept about a dozen chickens. I whined, sniveled, and cajoled my mother into buying me a blue one. I never did know how or when the dye process occurred—before or after hatching? So I took this little chick home and put it in the pen with the bigger chickens. They took turns chasing it around the pen, so they were playing and having fun. I checked later and found the little guy dead with his head a bloody mess. They pecked him to death. Perhaps because he was different. They were all white, and he was blue. They were older; he was younger? Whatever. Thank goodness people are smarter than chickens. Right?

Mr. Monroe lived in a much nicer neighborhood than ours. He was a banker and always wore a white shirt and tie. He owned a farm just outside of town. A nice tax write off. He was a deacon in our church, passed the collection plate, ushered, and helped with communion every Sunday. My mother used him as an example for my dad and me. Everyone has a peccadillo or two. Mr. Monroe had more than his share. My dad took me into the Piccadilly liquor store where he bought his daily half pint of whisky. We entered the front door. Mr. Monroe came in the back door from the alley. In all fairness to Mr. Monroe, his wife, who paid me my twenty cents every Saturday morning, looked like she was constipated or had a toothache.

I found that as a golf caddy, the richest men always had the biggest heaviest bags and usually tipped the least. One day I had the ultimate nightmare for a caddy. We were short on caddies. My number came up in the caddy shack. I was told to caddy double for Mr. Monroe and Ike Gilderbach. Ike was a hooker and Mr. Monroe was a slicer. They might as well have been playing alone, because they were never in the fairway together. I ran my legs off. At the end of a horrible 18 holes, they each tipped me a dime.

Back in the 1930's and 1940's, the Illinois state high school basketball tournament was held in a tiny gym that held perhaps 7,500 people. The Sweet Sixteen could easily have drawn another 15,000 fans, but no room for them. Each year, Mr. Monroe could be found standing on the corner outside the gym with a fistful of tickets that he scalped for much more than they were worth.

In later years when I had a paper route that included the red light district, I saw Mr. Monroe enter the back door of a particular favorite house. He always parked his car out of sight in the alley. His wife slept late on Sunday morning, so he arose early, dressed in his best suit, white shirt and tie to be ready for church. Then he visited his favorite women. He probably told his wife he had been out for breakfast with the boys. My guess was that perhaps she knew and didn't care. She was a very plain looking woman, and that is being very kind. Her father owned the bank that Mr. Monroe inherited. Nepotism comes hard sometimes.

One day I told my dad all these things I had seen regarding Mr. Monroe. I said, "Mom is always telling us to be like Mr. Monroe. Should I tell her all these things I know about him?"

"No, it would just upset her. Let her think the best. Remember, Son, not every person that goes to church is a hypocrite. There are a lot of good people out there."

"So he is someone we shouldn't be?"

"Someday he will have to answer to God. Just be yourself."

Bird feeding was not a big thing in the Thirties. You would have been looked upon as strange or even weird. There were no Wal-Marts, K-Marts, no special pet sections. People were lucky to feed themselves. Why would you want to feed the birds in those days? Songbirds were plentiful before the use of sprays like pesticides, herbicides, and the raping of the environment.

Mr. Monroe was into bird watching way before his time. He had a feeder and a birdbath in his backyard. I went down the alley behind his house and spied him holding a BB gun. This was unusual behavior for a grown man. "What are you doing, Mr. Monroe?"

"I'm shooting sparrows. There are too many of them. They get all the food before the pretty birds get it."

"Pretty birds?"

"Yeah. The finches, grosbeaks, cardinals. I even had a bluebird here once. I shoot those sparrows right off the feeder. I hate those damn sparrows."

At about that time, a powerful man in Germany was espousing the same ethnocentric philosophy. He would personally decide which people should live and who deserved to die. In my mind, I could see a lonely sparrow huddled on a tree branch wondering where his family and friends have gone.

My father gave me lots of good advice when I was a boy.

1. Never trust a man that wears a white shirt and tie to work.
2. Never trust a left-handed card player.
3. Never buy a Ford.
4. Never trust a man who won't take a drink.
5. Don't drink gin. That's a poor man's drink. (I later found if you add a splash of vermouth and an olive, it becomes a rich man's drink.
6. Watch out for "snake feeders". They are oversized wasps that bite and sting something awful. (I later discovered the dragonflies he referred to were beautiful harmless insects with large gossamer wings.)

At this same time, some mothers were showing their daughters how to cut off both ends of a cucumber and rub them on the remaining cucumber to remove the poison. Also some young girls, while having their periods, were not allowed to help with the home canning of peaches. If they touched the fruit it could spoil the entire batch. That must have made the girls feel rather special.

Mrs. Gehrke was a nice friendly old German lady that lived in the next block. When the weather was nice you could usually find her sitting in the front porch swing of her tiny white house. She would be reading or doing some sort of needlework. She asked if I would like to earn some money. Dumb question. She handed me two huge wicker market baskets and told me to go anywhere and pick just the blossoms of dandelions. The yards and vacant lots were loaded with them. She paid me five cents for each heaping basket. I asked why she paid me so much for these worthless yellow blossoms. She only smiled and said it was her secret.

Earlier in the spring my mother had me pick the tender leaves of the dandelions before the plants bloomed. She cooked them and we ate them like spinach. This was to thin our blood for the approaching summer. We also dug the roots of the sassafras tree for the same reason. We made tea from this diaphoretic. The fragrance filled the house like incense.

After being rewarded by Mrs. Gehrke, I figured that someone who had labored in the vineyards should know something about the grapes. So I asked my dad, who knew everything, "What does Mrs. Gehrke do with all those dandelions I pick for her?"

He explained, "She makes wine."

I was stunned. "How do you know this?"

"Because sometimes I trade her some of my homebrew beer for a bottle of her wine." These were clandestine operations at that time. Prohibition drove people underground. It failed miserably. The only thing it proved was, you can't legislate morality.

Mrs. Gehrig was a nice old white-haired lady that lived on our block. She lived alone and my mother told me that she had been kicked out of her Catholic church because she was divorced. I guess that was a big deal in those days. Once in awhile she would ask if I would like to go to a Saturday matinee movie. We walked eight blocks to this tiny theater in the worst section of town right next to the railroad depot. I don't know the real name, but the locals called it "The Bucket". The movies were black and white and there were no ushers. It had a single aisle between two rows of seats. There was a wooden ledge that ran along both walls. From the inside seats along the walls you could reach these ledges and set your popcorn on them. That is, if you didn't mind sharing it with a mouse or a cockroach. The big treat was going next door after the movie. The Greek confectionary was awesome. The décor was classic ice cream parlor. This is where I first experienced milk shakes, hot fudge sundaes, and especially huge banana splits. What a lucky kid.

Mrs. Gehrig had huge purple grapes in her back yard. She made wine and served me slices of warm homemade bread slathered with luscious grape jelly. My mother was not overly fond of Mrs. Gehrig. I made the mistake of telling her how wonderful Mrs. Gehrig's bread and jelly was. Mom's question was, "You like her bread and jelly better than mine?" I learned a cardinal rule of dealing with women at an early age. Especially when dealing with your mother or wife, do not praise another woman too much. When I was first married, my beautiful young bride made potato soup. Being Irish, it is one of my favorites. She had a great recipe and pureed the mixture. Again big mistake. I said, "This is really great. Love it. But my mother puts chunks and slices of potatoes in it." Dumb.

Her eyes narrowed and from across the table she said, "If you like your mother's potato soup better than mine, then go and have her make it for you." I spent the next fifty years of my life making my own potato soup.

One day I went to Mrs. Gehrig's house to sit beside her in her front porch swing and visit. She wasn't on the porch so I knocked at the door. No answer. I opened the door and smelled something awful. I found her in the kitchen. The gas jets were open on her stove. She was sitting in a chair in front of the open oven door. I ran to tell my mother. She said, "Oh, Wayne, you have such an imagination."

Why don't people ever believe me? Being the rotten selfish kid I must have been, my first thought was, "There go my cowboy shows and banana splits."

I must have been one of the first disciples of Hedonism. Seek pleasure and avoid pain? What's wrong with that? Pleasure being the ultimate goal of life? I've always enjoyed good food and drink.

I saved my money and bought my first bicycle. It was a used red and white bike with a big comfortable saddle seat, long wide handlebars, and balloon tires. It had only one pedal. The other one was broken off. Like people who name boats and ships. I gave it a name. Popeye was popular in cartoons. He only had one eye, and my bike had one pedal. Popeye was a perfect name.

My mother gave me some money and told me to run an errand for her. She gave concise instructions. "Go downtown to Mr. Buehler's Meat Market and ask for a pound of liver. Tell him it is for our dog. Then go to the creamery and buy two dozen cracked eggs."

I leaped on Popeye and headed downtown. There was no charge for the liver. Free liver for the dog? We ate the liver. I'm sure we were not aware that it was loaded with good biotin, and we certainly had never heard of cholesterol. Good old Mr. Buehler knew that his free liver for the dogs was supper for lots of poor folks.

It was eight more blocks to the creamery where I bought the two-dozen cracked eggs. No special container. The eggs were carefully placed in an ordinary brown paper sack. My bike didn't have a basket, so I had to be a very careful and skillful rider.

Now I'm heading downhill in the street when who do I spy walking on the sidewalk? It's Mildred with her girlfriend. What a golden opportunity to impress her. Even with just one pedal, it's downhill, and I'm really flying. Liver and cracked eggs be damned. I yell, "Hey, Mildred!" At that moment some guy opens the door of his parked car—I smash into it and sail over the handlebars. I don't know what hurt most, my hands and knees or the laughter from the girls. The front wheel was horribly bent. Oh, how I wanted to cry. The worst was yet to come. How do I explain this to my mother? Especially the big rip in my new pants. I hated those knickers anyway.

Since we lived by the railroad tracks, we had more than our share of hoboes. These hungry men, stripped of their dignity, always came to the back door. It broke my heart to see men looking for any kind of work, destitute, begging for food. Most of them got right to the point. A typical vagrant would say, "I'll eat anything you can spare." Hat or cap in hand, he would offer to work for a slice of bread or a glass of milk. My mother gave them apples from our tree in the fall, raw vegetables from the garden, cookies, and lots of lard and sugar sandwiches. In turn, they sharpened knives, mowed the lawn, washed windows, and shoveled snow. Those were the good old days?

At Christmastime, the local merchants gave free gifts to customers. Gas stations passed out road maps; furniture stores awarded heavy indestructible wooden yardsticks. Lumberyards presented big sturdy thermometers. I gathered mercury from broken thermometers in the alley and kept it in Prince Albert or Sir Walter Raleigh tobacco cans. I poured it on my desk at school and played with it when I was bored.

When I was in the sixth grade the music teachers held a citywide contest to see who could best identify classical pieces. From dozens of records, they would put the needle down on the Victrola and play just a bit or parts of the songs and we were to identify each on paper: Mozart, Beethoven, Strauss, Wagner, Bach, Tchaikovsky. I won the contest. Not bad for a sparrow in the stick section of Rhythm Band. I also began to take private lessons on the violin. I loved music.

A few men have been labeled as being handsome. I would put Errol Flynn, Robert Redford, Robert Taylor, and Tyrone Power in this group. And then there was Kelly. One hot summer, I hung around the Coca-Cola bottling plant. They kept a huge cooler filled with ice-cold bottles of Coke. Here is where I met Kelly. He was the best-looking young man I ever saw: chiseled features, green eyes, flashing white teeth, slim waist. I never knew if Kelly was his first or last name. It was embroidered in red over the pocket of his white shirt. I offered to help him load his truck, and my reward was a free Coke. He became my very first real boss. Twenty-five cents per day and my noon meal. There was no plastic and no aluminum cans. It was all glass bottles in heavy wooden cases. And no Child Labor Laws. I helped load the truck early in the morning and unloaded the empties that evening. Then during the day, we delivered to the stores, cafes, and bars. I carried out the empties and brought in the full cases. This offered Kelly the opportunity to take orders and flirt with the female employees. The ladies swooned and fell all over him. I swear he must have dated every woman in town. He would have made a great magician. His hands were moving all the time.

 I couldn't believe the places I had to go into where the pop was stored. Sometimes in locked sheds in the alley. Sometimes in dark damp basements. I battled rodents, insects, reptiles, and cobwebs while Kelly was making out with a waitress.

 The first day on the route, we stopped in a café for lunch. I had never eaten anything anywhere except in a home. I sat right up to the counter just like a little man and picked up a menu. Kelly asked, "What would you like, Big Guy?" I liked it when he called me that or referred to me as his assistant or his man.

 "What are you having, Kelly?"

 "I think I'll try a Canadian bacon sandwich, a bowl of soup, and coffee."

 I had never heard of Canadian bacon. I put the menu aside and said, "I'll have the same. Except I'd like a glass of buttermilk instead of coffee." I would never forget my first meal in a real café. I couldn't wait to tell my mother that evening. She was proud of her hard working little man.

 At the age of fourteen, I retired from the junk business and went straight. I got myself a paper route and tried to forget that Sam had taken advantage of a mere kid for the past three years. Anyway, at fourteen, I had graduated from the cowboy movies to more sophisticated films. I identified with Andy Hardy as he chased his girlfriend, Polly, through puberty. I laughed at the Marx brothers., W.C. Fields, and the Three Stooges. Buster Crabbe, as Flash Gordon, kept me on the edge of my seat. Deep down inside, I realized that no one would ever really go to the moon.

I had seventy-five customers on my paper route. The newspaper cost twenty cents per week. The office got fifteen cents, and I received a nickel per customer. This included a huge Sunday edition. In the Thirties, people didn't pay the office in advance. Each Saturday morning, I went door-to-door collecting. If a family moved out owing me for five weeks, I was stuck with the dollar. The office took its fifteen cents right off the top each week.

When someone moved into an empty apartment or vacant house on my route, I asked the new arrival about starting the paper. A new start not only meant another nickel per week for me, I was rewarded by a free pass to a movie at the Virginia, Rialto, or Orpheum. I had to go into the offices in the front of the News-Gazette to submit the name and address of the new start. The circulation department, where we peons received and folded our papers, was in the rear of the building. In between was the printing room. The printing room was off limits for the carriers. The machines were loud and dangerous. The men that worked there must have ended up deaf as rocks when they retired. I vividly remember that these men all made their own hats of folded newspapers. My friend and fellow carrier, Squirrely Jones, had access to the printing room, because his dad was a linotype operator. I used this relationship by brazenly walking through the printing department to get to the offices in front.

So, I'm on my way to collect a new start free movie pass. Lord, but it is so loud in this restricted room. I wave to Mr. Jones. People simply wave, nod, or use sign language. I open and close the thick heavy door behind me as I step into the hallway of the offices. The guy that issues the movie passes has an office at the far end of the hall. As I walk down the hall, I'm in awe of the plush carpet and impressed by the artwork on the walls. I peer through an open door into a room. There is a lovely young woman at her desk. I linger to gaze. She looks up, smiles, and motions with her hand for me to enter. She offers her hand over the desk. "Hi, I'm Marajen. What's your name?"

Tough question. I was tongue-tied by her beauty. "I'm Wayne."

"What route do you have?"

"Route 56."

"Let's see, that starts at Green Street on the north, First Street on the east, and extends to the west all the way to the railroad tracks?"

"How do you know this?"

"I know all the routes."

My mind is racing. Now I realize who this person is. This is the classic example of the sparrow and the bluebird. I am a 14-year-old 9th grader, and she is the 26-year-old daughter of the owner of the paper. She will soon become publisher and owner of the paper. I'm talking to my boss, "The Office". When she was 22, her father asked her to familiarize herself with all the departments and employees.

His advice, before he died in 1935 was, "Two things you must remember...never spend more money than you earn, and know there is no one so important you cannot live without them."

Before there was a jet set, this woman traveled the world on ocean liners. In addition to her local home, she owned a home in the Palm Springs, California area, and an Italian villa. She had longtime friendships with many celebrities including Loretta Young, Sir Lawrence Olivier, Mary Martin, Alice Faye, Phil Harris, Bob Hope, Peter Marshall, Guy Lombardo, Gary Cooper, and many others. Frequent guests at her Italian home were Loretta Young in particular and a number of political and military figures. Jacqueline Kennedy and her two young children were among others who visited.

Managing a newspaper was an unlikely role for a 22-year-old woman in the 1930's.

In 1941 she married Col. William Dyess of Texas, a pilot for the Army Air Force, who was captured by the Japanese when Bataan fell in April 1942. After a year in captivity, Dyess escaped. He was returned to the United States in 1943. He became a test pilot and was killed in an airplane crash. Dyess Air Force Base in Texas was named for him. His widely published account of the

Death March and the treatment of American POWs by the Japanese first brought that history to light.

She was known for her painting and philanthropy. She loved dogs and was a benefactress of the Champaign County Humane Society.

I was an awkward boy of 14 when this meeting took place with The Office. This was 65 years ago. I was so impressed by her humility, friendliness, and intelligence. She was indeed a lady that lived way before her time. Marajen Stevick. She died at age 90 in 2002.

Keep in mind: everything is relative. Compared to what? If you think you are so important you can't be replaced, remember this: your life on earth compared to all time is just a fleeting moment. The size of your funeral will probably be determined by the weather.

I couldn't believe the excuses my customers gave me for not having twenty cents. The most common was, "My husband forgot to leave me twenty cents today." A few paid a dollar for five weeks in advance. Some left the weekly money under a mat, in a flowerpot, in the mailbox. Sure did speed up collecting.

Old houses had big front porches.

I rode Popeye along the sidewalks and tossed the papers onto the porches. I folded the papers in two different ways depending upon the number of pages each day.

At Christmastime, it seemed the rich people were the most miserly and cheap, while the poor were inclined to be more generous. Most poor people tipped me when I collected just before Christmas. The tips ranged anywhere from a nickel to as much as a dollar. Many rich people never tipped at all. One year, the three richest people on my route collectively gave me an orange, a nickel, and a balloon left over from an early Christmas party.

The most coveted route in town was one that included a block of brothels. I don't think prostitution was ever legalized, but in the Thirties many towns had a street of houses where law enforcement never intruded. Ironically, our red light district was located on Church Street. Highly educated sociologists and psychologists have published research portraying prostitutes as miserable, unemotional, cold, unhappy, and neurotic. I tend to shy away from people who do research. If you copy from one source, it is called plagiarism. Copy from more than one, and it is called research. I believe Allport said, "When given a thimbleful of facts, people rush to make generalizations as large as a tub." We paper boys of the Church Street route found, contrary to published research, that the prostitutes were friendly, warm, and generous. We received more personal gifts such as handmade scarves and gloves. One of those terrible people gave me my first billfold. She hand stitched it and burned my initials into the beautiful soft leather. Another of those awful people remembered that I had told her that I loved to hitchhike ten miles to go fishing in the Sangamon River. And how I carried my fishing tackle in a tangled mess inside a cigar box. She gave me my first real tackle box. It had three folding trays. These women were much more likely to have me step inside on a miserable cold Saturday morning. And a few times I was led to the kitchen for hot chocolate and homemade donuts. I had never seen pancakes with blueberries in them.

The young girls on the school playground chanted rhymes as they jumped rope. One went, "Mabel, Mabel, set the table. Red hot pepper!" Another was "Stella, Stella, dressed in yellow, went downtown to meet her fella." I remember the names of three of the prostitutes: Mona, Kitty, and Stella. The Stella I knew had a special fragrance about her, sort of an aromatic redolence. A combination of vanillin and lilac. It was haunting. I felt a stirring in my loins. I didn't have the Church Street route long. The office replaced me with a younger boy. The office didn't need nor condone stirrings.

Part Two

World War II

Pearl Harbor signaled the beginning of the war for America. Loyalty and emotion ran high. On my eighteenth birthday I saw a movie called Wake Island. Shaking with rage and fired by patriotism, I enlisted in the marines with three of my friends. We had to go to Chicago to be sworn in. My dad, who was a railroad engineer, got us free passes to ride a train to Chicago. It wasn't first class. We shared the baggage car with piles of mail sacks and two coffins.

After being officially sworn into the marines, the recruiting sergeant wrote a note on a scrap of paper and signed it. He handed the note to me and said, "There is a little Greek café just down the street in the next block. It's called the Presto. Give this to the old guy in there and he will feed you a great meal. All your chow is on the Marine Corps now. You will catch your train for San Diego tonight. Semper Fi." We had never heard of Semper Fi, but we soon learned and never forgot what it means.

We found the Presto and presented the note. The old guy was working alone. He said, "Go sit down and I'll fix your food." He served us huge steaks with all the trimmings. As we were leaving he asked, "How were the steaks?"

"Fine. Great."

He then surprised us with, "I thought you might like to know that I feed all the new marine recruits horse meat."

I'll never forget my first meal as a U.S. Marine. I also couldn't know that the Japs would kill one of my companions within a few short months.

Our drill instructor at the San Diego Boot Camp was Sgt. Daly. The word was that he had seen duty in China. China marines have always been revered by all other marines of any era. Why, I really can't say. We respected and feared Sgt. Daly. One day he stuck his face within inches of mine and asked, "What is the serial number on your rifle?"

I don't know, Sir."

"You don't know?" he thundered. His eyes were a weird color, like those of a Weimaraner. His voice softened, nearly whispered, "I will ask you this again tomorrow. If you don't know the answer, I will personally take you out into the boondocks and hurt you real bad. Maybe kill you" I felt strongly that Sgt. Daly was a man of his word. I've always hated math. I'm terrible at numbers. I have a problem remembering my car license plates and even my phone number. But the serial number engraved on my rifle was 801272. Burned into my brain by those Weimaraner eyes.

While I was in the South Pacific, an election year came around. My outfit was made up mostly of young men from ages seventeen to twenty-three. Anyone in his late twenties or early thirties was invariably called "Dad". We were informed that anyone twenty-one or over could vote. I went to our company commander in protest. Our Captain Crawford was a marine's marine. He was feared, respected, and loved, nearly worshiped by our men. He was later killed by the Japs on Iwo Jima. A tragedy. A truly great young man.

"I would like to vote," I informed the captain.

"How old are you, Kid?" he asked.

"Nineteen, Sir."

"What the hell are you doing here taking up my time? You know damn well you can't vote. You're too young."

"Then send me home. I want to see my mom."

We exchanged thoughts for a few minutes. He could readily understand that I spoke for the majority of his company. He was a good officer. Sensing a morale problem, he offered me some of the officers' liquor ration. I immediately accepted the bribe. With my arms loaded with booze, I walked back to my young buddies. They stared in disbelief as I carefully set the bottles down. They had expected me to be court-martialed. Perhaps shot. When I related my story, they all cheered and pounded me on the back. The party lasted all night. I was a big man with my peers, but it was an empty victory. The captain had called me "Kid". After all, I wasn't a twelve-year-old selling junk to Sam. And nothing had changed, because I still didn't get to vote. I vowed to myself that since I couldn't vote now when I wanted to, needed to, deserved to...I would never vote again. I could see the headlines of the New York Times and Chicago Tribune. Wayne Barham Refuses to Vote. That would show 'em.

I shared a six-man tent with a handsome dashing marine from Chicago. He was a Polish lad named Zeke Kulbitski. When we last saw liberty in California and New Zealand, he always came back with exciting glowing tales of his adventures with beautiful girls. He had no problem gaining an audience, as we were always eager to hear anything about girls. One day after mail call, Zeke read a letter then smiled and sniffed it as if savoring the fragrance and put it under his bed. When he left, we did an awful thing. We dug out the letter and read it. I remember it verbatim.

"Zeke, my brother say he will kill you if he ever see you again. Send me the money you cheated me from. It's for you I've got it in. You kiss my ass that's what you are."

Of course we were sworn to secrecy not to tell him we invaded his privacy. He also was the first guy to get a corpsman to my side when I was wounded the third and last time.

I'll never understand how the Japanese thought they could conquer and then police and occupy the entire world. The very concept was insane. Let's say they did defeat the United States. Envision the occupation forces stationed in places like New York, Chicago, Houston, Detroit. A lone sentry wouldn't make it past the first dark alley.

People tend to forget that the day that will live in infamy (Pearl Harbor) also included attacks on Wake, Guam, and the Philippines. The Bataan Death March, a nine-day 55-mile horror, brought out the true character of the so-called honorable warriors of Japan. Their barbaric treatment and torture of prisoners was treacherous, dastardly, cowardly, sadistic, degrading, and unforgivable. The survivors were forced to work in coal and copper mines for three years in Japan. The men of Bataan sang a chant that they still remember today: "We're the battling bastards of Bataan, no mama, no papa, no Uncle Sam, and nobody gives a damn." Giant global corporations such as Kawasaki, Mitsui, Mistubishi, and Nippon Steel owned the mines. When American prisoners were finally released at the end of the war, our government gave them papers to sign swearing not to speak of the atrocities they had suffered. We were already suspicious of Russia and Red China. We wanted to covet the support of Japan. So after all these years, these powerful Japanese corporations have maintained that they don't owe anyone even an apology.

I remember 1944: The Third Marine Division returned to Guadalcanal from two months of combat on Bougainville. The veteran division had been camped since January in what I thought had to be the biggest coconut grove in the world. I was a nineteen-year-old Browning automatic rifleman with K Company, Ninth Marines.

Everyone remembers the infamous Axis Sally and Tokyo Rose from World War II. They are characters that history has recorded. We know who they were, what they did, and what happened to them. Conversely, anyone who spent time in the Solomon Islands was familiar with Washing Machine Charlie or Maytag Charlie as he was called. He flew a plane at night…never knew what time or where he would strike. The plane's engine sputtered and sounded like an antique that needed a tune-up. Where did he come from? From what base? How old? Never shot down? Like the Lone Ranger—who was this guy? A Jap hero?

It was June 2, and still dark, when we heard our last reveille on Guadalcanal. We walked from the grove, carrying full combat gear to Tetere Beach. A troop transport consisting of A.P.A.s, such as the Hayes, Jackson, Monroe, and Adams, floated offshore. On June 10, our convoy arrived at Kwajalein. We were shifted to LSTs and proceeded toward Guam on June 13. We cheered the news that Allied forces had landed in France.

Because of an anticipated naval battle at the time of the Saipan invasion, the Guam campaign was delayed. We became the floating reserve for Saipan. We went back to the Marshalls, putting in at Eniwetok. We remained for 27 days. We were impatient. We began to think we were going to rot there. W-Day for the liberation of Guam had been set originally for 3 days following the Saipan assault, presumably June 15. Hurry up and wait. The old game of the service.

A giant armada like Task Force 53 is an impressive, awesome sight. We had been aboard the LST 488 so many weeks, it seemed like home to us. The 488 looked like a toy compared with the battleships and aircraft carriers that loomed far above us as they passed. They actually bristled with firepower. They were ominously silent now, but they resembled huge dogs spoiling for a fight. It was reassuring to know they were on our side.

Before we returned to the Marshalls, our small troop convoy was separated from the larger vessels for a few days. We were told they were searching for the Japanese fleet that operated out of Truk. At dawn, four Japanese torpedo bombers attacked our small convoy. All four planes were quickly shot down into the sea. We marines stood topside and cheered like spectators at a football game. One of our ships was hit during the brief encounter. A plane made its run at an LCI, and I saw the torpedoes released. A forward gun crew was firing at the plane as it bore in on them. The entire bow of the LCI exploded. The men in the gun turret disappeared.

We had been aboard the LST 488 for weeks and were told that our food supply was running low. We were fed rations twice each day, morning and evening. The officers, meanwhile, ate three times daily. Their menu included such things as roast turkey with all the trimmings and freshly baked bread and pastries. We peered through the portholes into the officers' mess and saw blacks and Philippinos waiting tables set with silver and chinaware. It struck me that when the officers and enlisted men went swimming together in the nude we were all alike. As soon as we put our clothes back on, we lived in two different worlds. I volunteered for officers' mess duty so that I could steal pies and cakes and hand them through a porthole to my buddy. Later we would meet down below among the landing craft and eat our stolen prizes. It was like raccoons stealing sweet corn in the night. I smiled inwardly.

Guam. July 21. H-Hour, 0830. Task Force 58 had struck the airfields in advance of the invasion. Then Task Force 53 took over on W-Day. We watched the island being pounded from the air and sea. I thought it would surely sink. I had never seen rockets fired before. It was like the biggest Fourth of July fireworks display of all time. My stomach felt like it had a bowling ball rolling around inside. I felt sick.

We headed toward shore in a landing craft. At that time, our destination was known only as Blue Beach. Actually, Asan Point was on the right and Adelup Point on our left. We were in the first of 20 waves to land. I had been schooled in the use of the 50 cal. Machinegun, so I was at the gun while my mates crouched below. It seemed as though we were engaged in a giant race to see which craft would touch shore first. I was hoping we would be first, but we all appeared to hit the beach at the same time. I'm sure that hundreds of fat old bald-headed men today like to think they were the very first to hit the beach. I would wager that most of them are right.

There was an 8-foot embankment staring us in the face as we landed. I was last out of the landing craft. I jumped over the side into a foot of water. My helmet fell off my head and into the water. I reached over to retrieve it, but a huge wave washed it ahead of me on shore. I finally caught it and put it on. I looked up and down the beach and discovered I was all alone. My comrades had scrambled up the embankment and were gone. I climbed the bank and saw everyone running across 500 yards of open flat land to the base of a range of hills. I started in pursuit. I was halfway across the open ground, when a sniper opened up on me. I could see mud kicking up around my feet. Nothing sounds more frightening than the whine of ricocheting bullets. I was running fast and saw a huge shell crater ahead. I dived headfirst into it. I was in mid-air before I saw it was deep and partly filled with water. I climbed back up to the rim of the hole and looked around. Smoke filled the air. The acrid smell of gunpowder choked me. The trunks of trees, with their tops gone, stood naked. Twisted steel and shattered concrete were mute evidence of the remains of a pillbox.

Looking over my shoulder, I could see the second wave of marines approaching the shore. I had to get out of there in a hurry. I finally caught my platoon on top of the first ridge. My landing that day compared with the performance of a Sad Sack or Beetle Bailey.

The first night ashore we pulled back and dug in on that first ridge. We started taking heavy mortar fire. A shell landed so close, the explosion lifted my body right off the ground. My ears were ringing. Both my legs were wet and sticky with blood. In the darkness, I couldn't see, but I could feel holes in my pants where the shrapnel had ripped through. I thought I was bleeding to death. I later discovered that my canteen had been punctured. This extra wetness had added to my anxiety.

When morning came, my outfit moved out. They left me to be evacuated to a hospital ship. I waited on the beach to be transported. Suddenly, the Japanese began shelling the beach. Shells were bursting out in the water to my right. Then they moved in on the beach. The explosions began working their way along the beach toward me. It reminded me of probing fingers of death. I tried to dig under the sand, but there wasn't time. I lay flat on the beach, praying in every language and faith that I knew. A corpsman, holding a bottle of plasma high in the air stood over a wounded marine. I yelled for him to get down. The next shell killed both of them instantly. Another exploded and my ears were ringing again. It made me angry to know that I was about to die while feeling so helpless. I waited for the next explosion, but none came. A miracle? Blood was dripping down the back of my neck. I took off my helmet and stared at a small hole in the back. A larger and jagged hole came out the top. The fragment had only creased my skull.

The beach was littered with hundreds of gas masks. After all those hours of lecture, demonstration, and use of the gas mask, it was discarded the moment we hit the beach. Many were slipped quietly into the sea on the way in. Excess weight to carry.

On the hospital ship, I was told to stand up and hold on to the side of a bunk, while a doctor probed for the shrapnel in my legs. I was given wooden tongue depressor to bite on.

The next day, I was standing topside along the rail watching new casualties come aboard. A wild-eyed marine was hauled up and over the side. He fell to the deck and crawled around on all fours looking for a place to hide. He whimpered and made strange sounds like a frightened dog. He had seen his foxhole buddy beheaded by a samurai sword. The severed head had rolled downhill and stared up at him with open eyes.

I was released from the hospital ship on July 25 and told to return to my outfit. My legs were to be freshly bandaged each day. I was put ashore only God knows where late in the afternoon. It was getting dark. I decided to hole up for the night. I had no idea that the Japanese would pick the night of July 25-26 to launch their most fierce counterattack. It lasted all night long. There was gunfire all over the hills above me. Yelling, screaming, and confusion reigned. People were running all around me in the darkness. It was a nightmare. A dream that failed. When dawn came, I learned that groups of Japanese had broken through in isolated places. Some got down on the beach where they ran through some hospital tents. Some of the screams I heard came from the wounded marines being bayoneted in their cots. An estimated 3500 Japanese died that night.

It wasn't easy locating my outfit. K Company had pulled out and made a second landing on Cabras Island just offshore. They returned to the main island where I joined them. We moved across the island. Then we turned and began moving north.

The stench of death cannot be described. It must be experienced. The hot sun bloats bodies very rapidly. The flies swarm. Maggots wiggling in the eyes, ears, nose, and mouth. Not pretty. A crew of Seabees was loading dead Japanese onto a large truck. Two men grasped the ankles and wrists of a body. It reminded me of games we played at swimming holes when we grabbed someone and said, "One, two, three!" We made two false swings and threw the guy into the water on the third. In this case, the Seabees threw the body. The flesh came right off the bones of a hand causing the Japanese to crash head first into the tailgate of the truck. I doubt that he felt it. The Seabees swore.

I began to regard the enemy dead with unemotional contempt. Yet, I was compelled to search the features of all dead marines hoping not to find a familiar face. Death became a very personal thing. It only mattered if I knew the man. I sat down to eat my rations in the middle of dead bodies. Rigor mortis drew them into unbelievable grotesque positions impossible to assume in life. I used them as picnic tables on a Sunday afternoon. I sat with my back against a tree and placed my mess gear on the chest of one and my canteen cup on another. A cigarette case protruded from a pocket. I opened it and discovered a picture of Deanna Durbin inside. All this as I'm munching and drinking. How unfeeling can a man become? Today, I hear people complain to a waitress if they are served a glass with lipstick on it. Everything is relative. Compared to what?

We all began to look alike. Red dust caked our clothes and bodies when it was dry. Red mud did the same when it rained. We were haggard from lack of sleep and climbing hills. We never took our clothes off. I realized that I hadn't had my shoes untied for days. I once heard that Joe DiMaggio wore the same unwashed socks when he established the major league record for base hits in 56 consecutive games. No wonder. The catcher and umpire probably couldn't see.

On August 1, I lost the best friend I ever had. Jack Rich was killed when a Japanese hand grenade exploded between his legs. We had been buddies since we met back in the states. We had shared all the things that young men care about. Mainly, girls and dreams. Both of his legs were shattered. I touched them and they felt like a rabbit that had been shot at close range by a 12-gauge shotgun. He was still conscious and full of morphine. It was pouring rain, and his foxhole was full of water and blood. He looked up at me and smiled, "Don't cry, buddy. Remember to go see my mom and dad. Okay? It doesn't even hurt. Honest. Please don't cry."

They carried him down the hill. His legs were amputated. He was buried in Hawaii. I sat in that damned blood-soaked hole and sobbed for a long time. No one came near me. I kept repeating, "Why?" I don't even know where we were that day. We were on top of a mountain. What a price to pay for a mountain. It could have been Mount Tenjo, Mount Chachao or Fonte Ridge. My personal war consisted of cover. I lived from hole to rock to tree to cave.

We never knew where our orders came from. In a rifle company, "the word" is passed along verbally from man to man. We could hear it coming and then going down the line. Things like,

"Dig in, take 10, move out, chow time, smoking lamp is lit, take cover." Once I nearly fainted when I heard "the word" coming down the line. "Gas!" We looked furtively around, and there was one guy that still had his gas mask. Fortunately, "the word" proved to be false. I've always wondered what would have happened if it had been true? The scene could have resembled a pack of snarling dogs fighting over a bitch in heat.

I can't believe how unsophisticated I was at nineteen. I had never heard of Pearl Harbor before it was struck by the Japanese. Korea was also unheard of. My high school science consisted of playing with litmus paper. It was magic, because it turned a different color when you dipped it into certain liquids. No one ever told me why. Therefore, when I was informed that the Japanese had slave laborers of Koreans and Guamanians, I worried about shooting them by mistake. What do they look like? How can I tell? We only had to make that decision once. A huge number of Guamanians appeared over a hill and started coming toward our lines. We never knew where they came from nor where they went. Men, women, and children were laughing, crying, and waving tiny American flags. Where the flags came from will always be a mystery to me.

While on patrol we came to a fast, clear stream. We were hot, dry, and thirsty. We flopped on our bellies and drank our fill. We got to our feet and proceeded upstream. Not 10 feet from where we were drinking, the decomposed body of a Japanese soldier was lodged behind a log in the water. The stream gurgled noisily as it flowed over the entire body. Only his face protruded. The flies feasted. We couldn't miss seeing him as we passed. No one said a word.

I wonder if the wives and mothers of dead Japanese soldiers cry in the night? Hate lingers on after a war like the ashes of a flame burned out. No one really wins a war. Everyone loses. A pity.

The sunrises and sunsets in the skies over Guam must be unique. The earth was scarred, but the skies remained untouched. Sometimes the colors were unreal.

I walked quietly over a hill and came upon a Japanese soldier drawing a bucket of water from a well. His back was toward me. My grandmother had a well on her farm just like that one. She kept her butter and milk on a rope down deep near the water where it was cool. What a strange thought to have, as I squeezed the trigger of my B.A.R. He toppled forward headfirst into the well. I wonder if he is still there?

Covering a flame-thrower man was not a fun job. A B.A.R. man was assigned to throw rapid fire into caves. The object was to neutralize the enemy by pinning them down. The flame-thrower man worked his way as close as possible. Then whoosh! The smell of burning flesh and hair sickened me. It was worse than being downwind from a paper mill.

A marine walking directly ahead of me stepped on a land mine. It blew him into the air like a dummy in a movie. But this was real. Both of his legs were gone when he hit the ground. He pulled his body along the ground with his arms like a turtle when it walks. He never uttered a sound. He completed one small circle, before he pitched forward on his face in the red mud and died.

Fourteen days on Guam. I learned many things in two weeks. Don't walk along the top of a ridge against the skyline. Tracer bullets in an automatic weapon are pretty at night, but they give away your position and make you a popular target. A 30 caliber bullet makes a small dark hole the size of a pencil in a man's forehead, but the back of his head and his brains are gone. Bright pink blood, coming from the mouth in tiny bubbles, indicates a punctured lung. Red blood turns dirty brown when it dries. The screaming hiss of incoming artillery is terrifying. The same sound is gratifying if it is outgoing. I learned to hate war.

On August 3, we were walking along a road headed north. I stepped over, on, and around dead Japanese strewn everywhere. Colorful, exotic birds flashed in the branches of trees overhead. I stumbled along lost in a daydream of sharing a chocolate malt with a beautiful girl back in the states. My thoughts were abruptly ended by the staccato voice of a Nambu machinegun. Rifle fire and shouts added to the din of an ambush. I dived for cover off the road. I rolled over behind a dead Japanese and began firing with my B.A.R. across his chest. A very much alive Japanese burst out of the jungle and onto the road. He was 50 feet away and running straight at me. His weapon was a bayonet tied to the end of a bamboo pole. One burst stopped him. Smoke was curling up from the grass in front of me. I raised my head a bit and stared down into a hand grenade. Where the hell did that come from? I tried to roll away, but it exploded in my face. I could feel blood gushing from my face and ears. I was stunned but conscious. My entire head was numb. My war ended at that moment. I was blind. Someone was calling, "Corpsman." He was beside me in seconds. He said, "Grab my ankles with your hands and crawl out behind me."

We crawled for perhaps 50 yards. Then he sprinkled sulpha over my wounds and wrapped gauze around my head to keep the flies off my face. Soon there were other corpsmen around me. A voice said, "He's just about had it. Give him a shot of morphine, load him up, and get him out of here."

Strong arms lifted me into a Jeep. After a bumpy ride, I was transferred to a landing craft on the beach. The last thing I remember, before lapsing into unconsciousness, was being loaded aboard the hospital ship. I was flat on my back with my helmet on my chest. I clutched it with both hands. I poked my finger through the hole in it and said, "Please don't lose my lucky helmet. See, it has a hole right through the top. It's the only thing I want to take back with me."

A sailor assured me, "Don't worry about a thing, mate. We'll take care of it for you." I never saw it again.

I woke up in a hospital in the Russell Islands. Here is where I really faced reality. I was totally blind. I was confused, frightened, and angry. People told me how lucky I was just to be alive. Happy birthday, Wayne. Twenty years old and blind.

My new world was dark. It was filled with sound, touch, and fantasy. I found myself a bystander rather than a participant. At night, the rats came out and climbed around on the exposed rafters. The other patients flicked on the lights and threw shoes at them. The rats must have been huge. They woke me up squealing and fighting over an open can of peanuts by my bed.

A wounded navy corpsman was in the bed next to mine. He had been on Guam with the Third Marine Division. A Jap had shot him as he was giving first aid to a marine. The bullet entered the side of his head above his eye then went through the back of his nose down through the roof his mouth, broke his jaw on the other side and came out his neck. He, too, was totally blind. We visited briefly for a couple of days. His mouth was wired, so he spoke with difficulty. The nurses and corpsmen fed him liquids through a straw. I tried to cheer him up by telling him jokes and other funny stuff, but it hurt him when he laughed. The nurses told me to knock it off, but I thought it was worth a little pain to take his mind off the condition he was in.

After visiting for three days, we only knew each other as Dick and Wayne. To pass the time and make conversation, I mentioned that I liked to hunt and fish. He did too. I explained that as a kid I had hitchhiked to fish in the Sangamon River. The Sangamon is a long river. At least I knew it ran through Illinois. This got Dick's attention. He uttered, "I've fished the Sangamon."

"You're kidding. Where?"

"Near my hometown in Champaign, Illinois."

"Hey, that's where I'm from, too. What's your name?"

"Dick Bucher."

"My God, Dick. I'm Wayne Barham!"

We had gone to the same high school. He was one year ahead of me in school. His father was our family doctor and had delivered me as a baby. Dick was awarded the Navy Cross. He never regained any vision. When his father died, his older sister cared for him the rest of his life. I saw him a few years ago at a combined three-year class reunion. People begin to combine class reunions when Father Time speeds the attrition rate. Dick and I had much to reminisce. He never complained. He died shortly after our meeting. A true American hero.

Another hospital. This time on Guadalcanal. A doctor told me, "Your left eye has had some small shrapnel removed. There is a slight chance you might regain some vision there. Your right eye is all done. The optic nerve was destroyed. It is a little soft, so we might as well remove the eye. We'll do it tomorrow."

"No, you won't," I answered. "I'll wait until I get back in the states in a better hospital than this."

I remember having two teeth extracted during boot camp in San Diego. There was absolutely nothing wrong with the teeth. Someone had made a mistake on my examination chart, and they were marked to come out. I feebly protested, but two officers and two corpsmen threatened me. I was 18 and only two weeks into boot camp. The teeth came out, but I still have my right eye. I have no vision with it, but it is better than an artificial eye.

A group of officers came through the hospital awarding medals. I could hear the calls of "Attention, at ease, etc." The Entourage was moving in my direction down the ward. A high-ranking officer was surrounded by a flock of underlings. They stopped at the foot of my bed and someone snapped, "Attention!" I made no effort to get up. I heard a whispered, "Can he walk?"

"Yes, sir, but he's blind."

"On your feet, marine."

"What for?" I asked.

"You have a Purple Heart with two gold stars."

Propped up in bed, with my hands clasped behind my head, I began to laugh. It seemed ludicrous to be asked to stand at attention in my short hospital gown. It seemed appropriate that medals be awarded on parade grounds with bands playing. Using his voice as a guide, I stared at where his eyes might have been and said softly, "Just toss it on the sack here beside me."

I was pressing him and he fumed, "You're talking to a commander."

I answered, "I'm impressed."

He was in an awkward position. Young blind marines simply aren't shot nor even imprisoned. It would be like calling John Wayne a coward, walking on a grave, or insulting motherhood.

More whispering around me.

"What's the matter with him?"

"Poor attitude."

"He's been through a lot, sir."

I felt the medal plunk down beside me on the bed. The group moved on. About an hour later, I heard someone approach my bed. I recognized the voice of the same commander. This time he was alone. He said, "Wayne, I'm sorry."

He lit a cigarette and placed it gently between my lips. Then he took my hand in his and shook it firmly. It was good. Without another word he walked away.

The next stop was Mare Island, California. The flight across the Pacific was my first plane ride, but I couldn't see to enjoy it. It was midnight when we touched down in the U.S.A. At the hospital a nurse tucked me into bed and asked, "What would you like to eat? Just name it, and we will have it prepared for you."

The VIP treatment was a new experience. "You mean it? Really?"

"You bet."

I ordered a steak, French fries, tossed salad, strawberry shortcake, and milk. In less than an hour she was sitting on my bed feeding me strawberries. I don't know which I enjoyed most: the food or the special attention and perfume of a real live girl.

My weight was 180 pounds when we hit the beach on Guam. After climbing all those hills, little food, hot sun, and several days of unconsciousness, my weight dropped to 137. The sight of a blind, skinny marine must have brought out the maternal instinct in those San Francisco girls. I refused two proposals of marriage. Mothering really wasn't what I needed. I hated to leave San Francisco.

The Philadelphia Naval Hospital was my final home in the Marine Corps. It was October when Commander Duane Beam performed the surgery on my left eye. After the operation, I had to lie flat on my back with my head between sandbags for three days. Then came the moment of truth. The patients and nurses crowded around to watch as the bandages were removed. I held my breath. I only hoped for enough vision so that I could get around by myself without being a burden.

I could see light, color, and movement but everything was blurred. Commander Beam explained he had removed the lens from my eye. He handed me a large magnifying glass with a handle on it and said, "Tell me what you see through this."

I couldn't believe it. Everything cleared up. I looked into the faces of complete strangers all around me. Yet I had known all these people for several weeks.

"I can see you," I exclaimed.

They all cheered and applauded. The tension was broken. Everyone was jabbering. I held up one hand for silence. It was like conducting an orchestra. I explained, "I have to hear your voice to associate it with your name and face. One at a time now."

There is no way to describe an experience like that. Holding my large magnifying glass close to my eye, I looked into each happy face as they introduced themselves. It was a fun game. My mental image of everyone had been terribly inaccurate. A blind person could make anyone look beautiful or ugly in his mind. The only criteria used in judging people came from how they treated me as a human being. I had become an astute judge of character, because physical appearance was unimportant. The length and style of hair, beard, mustache or color of skin meant nothing. This entire concept is reversed with people who can see. A pity.

Before that day ended, I walked to a window and looked out over a park down below. The October leaves were yellow, orange, and red. I had waited nearly three months to see them. It was like being reborn all over again. That night, I took my long-handled glass down the hall to where a film was being shown. It was *The Good Earth*. I agreed.

A week passed. I was wearing my new glasses when a dark-haired, handsome French sailor was admitted to our Ward 2-C. He was off a submarine. He couldn't speak English, and I couldn't speak French. Strangely enough, we both knew enough German to communicate. He was embarrassed to be in such a huge hospital with so many wounded men from combat. He was only having his tonsils removed. The male ego.

One night I took him to the roof of the hospital. The lights of Philadelphia were rather impressive from that height. There were tears in his eyes and he spoke with difficulty. He explained that this was the first time in several years he had seen a city with its lights on at night. He hoped to see France this way again some day.

He eagerly accepted my invitation to get a closer view of the city. There was one small problem. I had been restricted to the hospital for enjoying too much nightlife. The well-meaning doctors claimed it was for my own good. They said they were protecting and resting my eye. They had done this before, but I had gone into town anyway. This time, to ensure the restriction was adhered to, they confiscated my marine dress uniform. In the interest of international relations, I was forced to borrow a sailor's uniform. My French friend and I were soon drinking wine in a Jewish-American Legion Club. Drinking wine was a way of life with him. It was new to me. I remember leaning against the wall in the john trying to figure out how to unbutton the complicated maze of 13 buttons on my sailor's pants. Too late.

We stopped off into a sleazy nightclub for one last glass of wine. A fight broke out. A marine from Ward 2-C lost his artificial eye in the melee. We never did find it. The Shore Patrol was nice enough to escort us back to the hospital. The doctors were unhappy with me again, but they were an understanding group. The only unreasonable person was the sailor whose uniform I had borrowed. He was upset, because I had wet his pants. He wasn't too pleased with the large hole in the right knee either. What a poor sense of humor.

It was mid-December when the doctors sent me home on my first ten-day leave in over two years. The newspaper reporters greeted me in my hometown. They called me a twenty-year-old marine hero, complete with Purple Hearts and assorted medals and ribbons. I certainly was no hero...more of a survivor. The newspapers ran stories and pictures of the "Jap Killer" as they dubbed me. Wherever I went, old men shook my hand, old ladies bought me drinks, and young girls cast approving glances my way. It was embarrassing at first, but I soon got over that. It was flattering.

It was three days before Christmas as I walked along the street that led downtown. The snow crunched underfoot. Huge snowflakes wafted down on my green marine overcoat. I stopped to examine closely the individual snowflakes against the dark background of my sleeve. The unique geometric designs of snowflakes had always fascinated me, and I hadn't been in snow for over two years. This was a completely different world in contrast to the hot rotting jungles of the Southwest Pacific. I took a deep breath of cold December Illinois air and then exhaled sharply. I could see my breath. It was a simple thing, but I chuckled as I thought of those island natives. They would never experience the magic of seeing their own breath. As I stood contemplating life's complexities, I heard the voice of Bing Crosby singing "White Christmas". The music was coming from a loudspeaker over the door of the music store. I walked to the corner, stood under the loudspeaker, and hummed along with Bing until the song was over. When I turned to cross the street, a sign with an arrow pointing to my right confronted me. The sign read "Sam's Salvage".

It was likely a combination of many things. No doubt Bing Crosby, fresh white snow, and Christmastime played a part in it. I followed the arrow and found myself standing in front of the gate looking into the junkyard. Same old clutter. Same old scales. I recognized one of Sam's old workers. He had a gimp leg that caused him to walk like a stepped-on toad. He did a double take as he spied me standing at the open gate. "Hey, you guys! Look!" he exclaimed. "It's the Jap Killer."

He hopped over to the shack that doubled as Sam's office, pushed the door open and yelled inside, "Come see who's here."

A bald head with horn-rimmed glasses appeared at the open door. "Hi, Kid. Come on in."

I followed Sam inside and closed the door behind me. He held out his grimy old paw and we shook hands. He offered me a broken chair as he walked around his desk and sat down. "What brings you here, Kid?"

I reached into my front pocket and pulled out a very small roll of bills. I picked out a twenty and tossed it onto the desk between us. Before I could speak, Sam intervened, "You shouldn't carry your money loose in your front pocket, Kid. You might lose it."

I wanted to begin by giving him hell for cheating me out of all that money in the past. Instead, I bit my tongue and calmly stated, "Remember when I used to come in here with my little red wagon and sell junk? Well, I started out with good intentions, but somehow things changed."

"What things, Kid?"

I shifted uneasily in my broken chair. "Well, remember how you always piled scrap iron outside the high fence on the east side? I used to carry my wagon across the tracks and load it up and then pull it around through the gate. You weighed it and paid me. Hell, Sam, I was selling your own junk back to you. I figure twenty bucks should just about cover it. Okay?"

He turned his swivel chair around and stared out the window. I watched him as he pulled a handkerchief from his hip pocket. He took off his glasses, blew his nose, and put the glasses back on. Then he spun around and faced me again. I was growing uneasy. He picked up the money and folded it in half. Then he rose and walked around the corner of the desk to where I was sitting. He put his arm around my shoulder and slipped the twenty dollars down inside my shirt pocket.

"Keep it, Kid," he croaked. He cleared his throat and continued. "I appreciate your telling me this. I know it wasn't easy. Now let me tell you something. That big fence on the east side has knotholes in it. I realized how poor you were and how you needed the money for your cowboy shows. We used to get a kick out of watching for you every Saturday morning. The first guy that spotted you coming would signal the rest of us. We used to line up on the inside of the fence and watch you through the knotholes. It was so damned hard to keep from laughing out loud. I was just donating a dime for the cause. You were the only funny thing that ever happened to us around here, Kid."

I was stunned. Sam went back to his desk and tried to open the bottom drawer. It stuck. He gave it a good kick with his heel and then pulled it open. He removed a big brown bottle with a cork in it. "Would you have one drink with me?"

"You bet I would," I answered, "but you could get into trouble. I'm not legally old enough to drink."

"That's got to be the dumbest thing I've ever heard. You're the Jap-Killer. You're a hero."

"I know, but twenty-year-old heroes aren't old enough to drink."

Sam smiled, shook his head, and pulled the cork from the bottle with his teeth. He poured two coffee cups full of homemade Jewish wine. It was excellent stuff. We drank the entire bottle.

I stood up and put my heavy green G.I. overcoat on. We shook hands and looked deep into each other's eyes. I walked to the door and said, "You know, Sam, I think I'll turn you in to the police for giving booze to a minor." We enjoyed a good laugh together.

I opened the door and stepped outside. The cold air was a sudden shock, but the wine had warmed my insides. It was snowing harder, and the flakes were much larger. Once more I stopped to peer at the white geometric crystals on my sleeve. The voices of the Andrews Sisters floated on the wind from the corner music store. They were singing, "Don't Fence Me In", as I glanced at the east fence of the junkyard.

After I had walked perhaps ten paces, I heard the office door squeak open behind me. "Merry Christmas, Kid."

Without turning around, I said, "It isn't even your people's Christmas, Sam."

"I know, but Merry Christmas to you anyway."

"Merry Christmas to you, too, Sam," I called back over my shoulder as I walked away. I could feel wetness on my cheeks. Damned tears. I was careful not to let him see my face. After all, a twenty-year-old hero can't drink, can't vote, and can't cry. Everyone knows that.

My mind goes back to December 1944. My final discharge papers came through before my 21st birthday. I couldn't legally vote. I couldn't legally buy a glass of beer with "adults". While standing on a downtown Philadelphia corner, I overheard two men in their fifties talking. One of them said, "The next thing you know these young kids will think they have the right to vote. Now what the hell does a 20-year-old kid know about life anyway?"

Jack Rich never reached his 21st birthday. He died on a mountain on August 1, 1944. He was an alumnus of the university where I have been teaching for several years. His parents donated his casket flag to be used each October for our homecoming football game. It is a very special and particular flag. It touches the top of the pole just as the Star Spangled Banner ends. The crowd roars its approval. The kick-off shifts attention back to the field. The tears are dripping from the tip of my nose. I hope no one notices. Marines aren't supposed to cry. Everyone knows that.

PART THREE

Educational Potpourri

My three years as a student in Champaign High School were rather inglorious. I graduated 196 in my class of 212. We had an excellent school. My class rank bears out the prophesy of my Colonel Wolfe Elementary School. I was indeed a sparrow. Our high school had the first driver education program in the state of Illinois. I didn't partake. We also had an indoor swimming pool that I loved. Mrs. Gehrig was the cleaning lady for a rich jewelry storeowner, and his wife paid my membership to the YMCA where I learned to swim at an early age. I remember in swimming class, before the teacher supervised, we threw a black kid named Melvin into the deep end of the pool. He couldn't swim and sank to the bottom of the pool. But he held his breath and walked across the pool and pushed up to the other side. Terrible. We loved Melvin and would have saved him from drowning.

The thing I hated most about math and science was that I never had a teacher that ever told me why or how I could use this information. We dipped litmus paper into solutions and they turned red or blue or whatever? So what? Magic.

I hated algebra and geometry classes for the same reasons. Too bad Bill Gates hadn't arrived with his famous quote, "Be good to the nerds in your class, because you probably will end up working for one of them."

Miss Cunningham taught geometry. Her only goal in life was to make me miserable. She would say, "Wayne, put number four on the board." I might have spent an hour on number four...no matter; I never understood any of it. She would then proceed to say things like, "Wayne, you really work at being stupid. I can see you never even looked at this assignment." God, I hated her. It is really fun to be a 16-year-old and be humiliated in front of your peers. I usually hit the boys' bathroom and threw up before 6th hour geometry class.

My history teacher never got as far as the Civil War. As a junior in high school, the Boston Tea Party, etc. didn't turn me on. Of course we didn't have educational visual aids and interesting movies. Old Blinky, as we called him, was so boring I thought he had been embalmed and propped in front of the class. He did have one reputation. Most teachers assigned seats for roll taking by alphabet. Blinky, a nervous habit, always seated the best-looking girls with short skirts in the front row. He was rewarded for his boredom and 40 years of teaching by having a new elementary school named for him after his death.

When I was in junior high, excuse me—middle school—I was the best violinist in the orchestra. Quite a feat having played nothing but the sticks in elementary school. Sol Cohen and Mendel Riley had my schedule arranged so that I could ride my bike across town and play in the high school orchestra. It was the only time I ever felt comfortable among the robins and bluebirds.

The best part of being a student at the U. of Illinois was the athletic teams. The Illini ruled the Big 10 in football, basketball, and track, and they beat UCLA in the Rose Bowl in 1946. In those days, teachers took roll, and students were only allowed two or three unexcused absences. Some classes were huge, jamming a lecture hall with several hundred students. Seats were assigned and graduate students stood at the back of the rooms with clipboards and seating charts. I made money by prostituting myself. I hung out in the Student Union and let it be known that I was available to fill their seats if they wanted to cut a class. They told me the building, room number, row, seat, and time. I then took my own homework and did it at the same time I was getting paid. I lived at home, but some of the rich kids who lived in the frat houses had their own files of tests including midterms and finals.

It made it easy when they had the tests of teachers too lazy to make out new ones.

My foxhole buddy and I often talked of returning to his little town to play football after WWII. When he was killed, I still thought about it. My bride and I moved to Springfield, South Dakota, where I enrolled in little Southern State Teachers College. Quite a change from living in a large city and attending the huge University of Illinois. We soon knew everyone in town and at the college.

People were excited about the football prospects. Several good players were returning. Jack Martin was an excellent coach. I only had one eye and had to wear thick heavy glasses. No facemasks in those days. I sold Coach Martin on the idea that I could help the team by being the kicker. He was hesitant about my eye and glasses, but after I showed him how well I could kick, he said, "You are our kicker." Coach Martin had nicknames for his players. I was dubbed Radar because of my glasses. Other players were called Clank, Cub, Ike, and Tippy. Our co-captains were Dynamite Sazama and Big Dog Ferwerda. We were a mix of older married vets and young guys right out of high school. Our quarterback was a talented Indian right out of the local high school. Dick Drapeaux was the most talented quarterback I ever saw anywhere at the small college level. He was big, strong, tough, intelligent, and easily the fastest guy on the field. I was impressed by his poise. Even though surrounded by older teammates, there was never a doubt about who ran the offense. He knew the assignments for every position on the team. He was so quick: rifle-armed; a great passer, fierce competitor, and he had fun. I was in awe of the skills that God had given him. Came from a dreadful home, so his grandmother raised him. He was voted into the South Dakota Hall of Fame and the National Indian Hall of Fame.

Everyone loves a winner. It didn't take long to see that the 1949 Southern football team was a winner. This small college didn't have end zone seats in the football stadium. To accommodate the overflow crowds, the old and infirm were allowed to park their cars inside the stadium at both ends of the field. Tailgating hadn't been discovered in 1949, but fans showed up hours before kickoff time to get a good spot. Both end zones behind the goalposts were packed with cars. Teams from all the big schools were not used to this. Had never experienced it. A first down or a good play of any kind set off a blare of car horns and flashing lights from the end zone cars. Keep in mind, the stadium was packed and the overflow crowds were allowed to walk the sidelines. When a good pass reception, pass interception, good defensive play was made, there were the usual accolades of the cheerleaders, the people in the stadium, and the cars ringing the end zones. One thing in 1949 that you didn't see was individual displays of "Look what I did!" And when touchdowns were scored, the player tossed or handed the football to the closest official and probably said, "Here you go, Sir." No strutting, dancing, chest pounding, trash talking, look-at-me crapola.

That 1949 Pointer team became the first team to beat Yankton College in the history of our school. This team also won its first South Dakota Intercollegiate Conference championship, and was Southern State College's only undefeated team. It was fun to watch the big schools from the big cities come to town and ride down our single block of business on Main Street. They actually laughed at the thought of playing this tiny college. Those same teams very quietly got on the bus for the trip home after being whipped by scores like 20-0, 21-0, 27-0, and 49-7. It gave me such pleasure just being part of this scene. I only wished that Jack Rich could have been with us. Somehow, though, I felt that he was.

I enjoyed the small classes. I took an advanced grammar course from old Arch Crawford. He became my all-time favorite teacher. The class was so small he could put us all at the chalkboards at the same time. Then he would lean back, make up sentences, and have us parse them on the board. He could challenge the best students and have the patience to tutor the slower students. Unlike my high school geometry teacher who always had a fresh supply of venom to strike with, Professor Crawford always showed compassion.

Professor Gould was a character. He could speak five different languages and taught art and music. He also was the band director. One day he walked into his classroom and said, "I suspect there has been some cheating going on in this class." He proceeded to pass out new test papers for this day. Then he announced, "I can assure you there will be no cheating today." With that, he picked up a chair and put it on top of his desk. Then he climbed on top of the desk and sat in the chair. He folded his arms across his chest and looked down on his class. "You may begin."

Five minutes later, he fell sound asleep. Students whispered answers, checked crib notes, and silently departed. When he awoke, the room was empty and the papers were on his desk.

My first teaching job was in Central High School in Aberdeen, South Dakota. I taught four classes of social studies and was head football and basketball coach of the juniors who competed in a conference of smaller high schools. I also was assistant track coach of the varsity in the spring. My yearly salary was $2,750. Today coaches are hard to come by. Even small high schools advertise for assistant coaches, no teaching at all, just show up after school for practice and for perhaps $2,500, nearly my annual salary in 1950 for four classes and three sports.

I vividly remember that year of 1950-51 when we were hosting the State "A" basketball tournament in our high school arena. It was probably the biggest gym in the state at that time. Our teachers were to be assigned various tasks for the 3-day event. I went to Cy Holgate, our principal, and informed him that I didn't want to sell or take tickets or guard outside doors. I wanted to see and enjoy the games. Cy was a very good school administrator. "Let me think about it."

The next day he handed me a scorebook and said, "I'm giving you the best seat in the house. You are the official scorekeeper." I didn't tell him I had never kept a scorebook for a basketball game in my life. I found myself between the two teams on the floor with all the sportswriters with typewriters right behind me. No TV in those days. Some of the sportswriters were silver-haired legends from all over the state. Everything went well. Just once the scoreboard and my scorebook didn't jibe. A short respite and some quick help from the press and the problem was resolved. At the end of the school year, I received a phone call from Harvey Van Beek, the superintendent at Springfield High School. He offered me the job for next year, 1951-2 as head coach of all sports, four classes and Principal for $3,300. We are talking big bucks here. A raise of $550! When I was a senior at

Southern, I came down to the high school and was assistant coach for no salary, started American Legion baseball, and taught a high school Sunday school class. I also did my student teaching there. Mr. Van Beek drove up to Aberdeen, 200 miles to visit with me about the job. I had ordered a hindquarter of beef from the Aberdeen locker plant. It proved to be so tough we could barely eat the hamburger. So when Harvey and his wife drove into our driveway, I'm feeding our Springer spaniel a big T-bone steak. He looked at this in disbelief and said, "I'm not sure you really want to leave here...?"

A few days later Mr. Holgate called me to his office. He said, "You have done an excellent job for us this year. I'm offering you a contract for $3,000 for next year. But we expect you to start work on your Master's this summer." With a contract already in my pocket, I looked him in the eye and said, "Thanks, but Dorothy and I have lived frugally, and we plan to take a year off and go on a world cruise."

Speaking of dogs, we had been kicked out of our basement apartment because I had a beautiful Springer spaniel flown in from a kennel in Ohio. We named him Sniffer. We rented the first house we had ever lived in from an old couple that wintered in Florida. There were no leash laws so we would let Sniffer out two or three times each day. One day he came home wet with a wet chicken in his mouth. The chicken was alive and unharmed. I was at school, so Dorothy put the chicken under a washtub in the garage. We had no idea where the chicken came from. So what do you do with a live chicken when you are raking in $2,750 per year? We ate it. Next day, the same scenario. Another wet dog and wet chicken. I get in the car and drive all around the neighborhood. Three blocks down the street a creek flows by the backyard of a house. There is a chicken pen on three sides behind the garage with the fourth side open because of the stream. Chickens don't swim, but Sniffer does.

We lived about a mile from the school. When the weather was especially nice, I enjoyed leaving the car at home and walking to school. On one of those days, I was in the middle of my second period class when 30 kids burst into laughter. I turned and looked to where they were excitedly pointing. Right beside me sat a happy, panting, tail-wagging Springer spaniel. As a peace offering, he held out his paw to shake hands. What a show-off. What a ham. He got to shake hands with dozens of kids that day. This dog had tracked me a mile down sidewalks, across streets, into the school, and down the hallway right up to my desk. How do they do that?

Sniffer made the school newspaper. A girl wrote, "Mr. Barham's classes were treated by the presence of a special guest. He was the cutest guy in school" After doing his detective work, for which administrators get the big bucks, Mr. Holgate was not amused.

My wife of 55 years reminds me that during that first year of raking in the big cash as a teacher, South Dakota has always ranked 50th in teacher salaries, she squandered six dollars on herself. She bought two corduroy skirts, one red and one blue, for three dollars each.

I also remember the school year of 1950-51. The Yankees beat Philadelphia in the World Series. On TV it was the L.S.M.F.T. Lucky Strike Hit Parade. Groucho Marx's "You Bet Your Life" and on June 27 the U.S. entered the Korean War 'Police Action'. Humphrey Bogart was a hit in "The African Queen" and General McArthur was relieved of his command when Truman said, "Fire the sonofabitch."

Making friends with custodians is the smartest thing any school person can do. Upon moving back to Springfield, I was already familiar with the location of the coach's office. It was in the basement of the gym. It had a side door entrance. The gym was built by one of Franklin Roosevelt's work projects. The gym floor was made of beautiful wood squares. It was the pride and joy of our custodian, Herman Schultz. I walked a few blocks from home to the school to check out my office. I heard a scream, a shout, a howl from upstairs. It was a beautiful summer day; Mr. Schultz had the main front doors open and he had just finished putting some sort of a seal on the floor. I bolted up the stairs and met Sniffer coming down the stairs. He had tracked me from home and walked right down the middle of the still wet gym floor. Mr. Schultz was usually rather unemotional, even stoic, Have you ever seen a German with smoke coming out his ears and fire in his eyes? Not pretty.

My basketball team needed new warm-ups. Al Paulsen, the band director wanted a new French horn. He went to Mr. Van Beek with our requests. He informed us that he couldn't afford both, so would one of us yield to the other? No. This is why the school administrators get the big bucks. They make major decisions. Mr. Van Beek opted for the French horn.

A music contest was to be held at South Dakota University in Vermillion. I was delegated the task of taking a load of students in the driver education car.

We were to leave for Vermillion before dawn. I got my sleepy students into the car. "Okay, everybody in? Instruments and music in the trunk? Forget anything?"

"We're all set, Coach."

I back away from the curb and hear and feel a sickening crunch. What in the world? It's the new French horn. Al Paulsen and I became lifelong friends, but more than once, he accused me of doing this dastardly deed on purpose.

I was coaching in Robinson High School in Illinois in 1953-54. The Yankees beat Brooklyn. Eisenhower was inaugurated January 20. Nixon was vice president. July 26, 1953 armistice was signed at Panmunjon. It provided for a demilitarized zone along the North and South Korean boundary. The Nobel Prize in literature went to Ernest Hemingway for "The Old Man and the Sea" and "A Farewell to Arms". Henry David Thoreau's "Walden" was banned from U.S. Information Service libraries and labeled downright socialistic.

Robinson was known for two things at that time: the home of the Heath candy bar, and the author, James Jones. I received conflicting stories about young James from his former teachers. I'm not sure if he was asked to leave Robinson High School or if he chose to. At any rate, several teachers claimed they saw promise in him. He joined the army and later wrote about his duty when he was stationed at Pearl Harbor. I heard that he sent his manuscript out anywhere from twelve to twenty times before some publisher decided to take a chance that someone might like to read it. All those rejection slips...it makes me wonder who reads the manuscripts submitted to book companies. Especially the unsolicited ones shoved under the door and tossed over the transom. I'm talking about Jones' *From Here to Eternity*. The book was a best seller and the movie wiped out all the Academy Awards that year. To this day, it remains one of my favorites.

In the mid 1950's we moved to northern Wisconsin where I became the football coach at Rhinelander High School. The team had been terrible during the past two years. Morale was low. The seniors had never won a game. I admired them for showing up for their last season of football. I remember practicing before our first game. We were working on kicking extra points. I sensed some horseplay and asked why they thought something this important should be funny. The answer was, "Coach, we have only scored 7 touchdowns in the past three years. We don't get to kick many extra points."

The Wisconsin Valley Conference was split into two divisions that year. We won the Northern Division. We also won back the Hodag Bell, a traveling trophy with our big rival Antigio. Our students had never seen it. The scores of all previous games were engraved upon it. And now, fifty years later, these two schools still battle for "The Bell".

In 1956 we built a cabin on Oneida Lake ten miles west of Rhinelander. It nestles on 250 feet of shoreline. At that time, the fishing was fantastic. I walked the shoreline in chest waders using a fly rod with a popper in the spring. Crappies were plentiful with some up to 18 inches long. Most people have never seen a foot-and-a-half crappie.

The colors of Wisconsin's North Woods rival those of New England in October. Not simply red and yellow, but bright orange, crimson, and gold. At this time of year it's hard to beat the smell of wood smoke trailing upward from the fireplace with steaks on the grill outside (charcoal of course) and a Wisconsin brandy manhattan in hand.

During the late 1950's, those Damned Yankees were beaten by Brooklyn, then the Yankees beat Brooklyn, Milwaukee beat the Yankees, and the Yankees beat Milwaukee. Jonas Salk developed a polio vaccine available on a mass basis. The novel *Peyton Place* was a best seller.

I've never forgotten the day that Mr. Van Beek drove into my driveway in Aberdeen and offered me the position as teacher, coach, and principal at tiny Springfield High School. He said, "You will have to meet with the school board, and they may or may not approve this. You know, of course, that the biggest church in Springfield does not approve of drinking, smoking, or dancing. They pretty much set the tone for the culture of the surrounding area. The board members will ask you questions relating to these personal things. You had better have the right answers. Do I make myself clear?"

I did smoke at the time and enjoyed a cold beer once in awhile on a hot summer day. I searched Harvey's face. "Are you telling me to lie?"

This was the most honest, truthful, conscientious school administrator I ever knew. Mr. Integrity. He shook his head. "I'm not telling you to do anything. What part of this don't you understand? I want you for my coach."

So, I found myself at the school board meeting. First question, "We have been told that you were seen going into Tom's Pool Hall when you were a student at Southern. Is this true?"

The pool hall sold beer. I answered, "I went in there a couple of times because I enjoy playing pool."

Next question. "Do you smoke?"

"No," I lied.

"Do you drink?"

"I had a beer or two when I was in the marines." An understatement and rather evasive. "I can remember when we were in the Solomon Islands, I was too young to vote or buy a beer. The Marine Corps issued us two bottles of beer or coca-cola. The Mormans in our company sold theirs for ten dollars a bottle. It was against their religion to drink it, but they accepted it and sold it."

This was met by silence. After an awkward period of time, the school board president proclaimed, "We respect Mr. Van Beek's opinion and will approve his request. However, you are not to go into the pool hall again, and if you are seen smoking or drinking your contract will be terminated."

While I was enjoying my job with some of the nicest young high school kids, my young wife walked downtown one warm spring day to pick up our mail at the post office. No problem? She wore a pair of red short shorts as they were called, and Mr. Van Beek was told to inform the coach that perhaps his wife shouldn't walk downtown dressed like that.

Four years later, I was offered an opportunity I couldn't refuse. I was hired as football coach in the beautiful Northwoods of Wisconsin. Rhinelander High School was a member of the prestigious Wisconsin Valley Conference. The town was predominately German and Polish. That fall, just before school started, my wife and I were invited to join the superintendent, principal, and school board for a dinner at one of the many great supper clubs in the area. This was the school board's way of welcoming all the new teachers. Martinis, manhattans, wine, prime rib. My wife and I will never forget that special evening. The entire tab was picked up by the school board members.

Everything is relative. Compared to what?

Part Four
Two Different Worlds

It is 1960. The population of the United States is about 180,000,000 people. The Federal Drug Administration has approved the first public sale of contraceptive pills, Enovid, at $10 for a month's supply. JFK has defeated Nixon. Last year, Alaska and Hawaii became the 49th and 50th states. Castro overthrew Batista. And we don't know that next year Roger Maris will hit his 61st homerun in the last game of the season to break Babe Ruth's 1927 record.

I am a teacher. I recently surprised my wife when I announced that we were going to attend the Charity Ball on Saturday night.

"Are they giving us the money it raises?" she asked.

"Of course not. I paid ten dollars for these tickets. We'll just have to take the ten from some unnecessary part of the budget."

"You mean like food, clothing, and house payments."

I ignored her sarcasm. Dorothy is a good wife and mother, but she doesn't understand high finance. Handling huge sums of money, like my monthly paycheck, overwhelms her.

"As a matter of fact," I continued, "there is a rumor floating around that the school board is going to hand out merit pay next year. All the board members will be at the Charity Ball. I figure I can visit with them, so they won't forget I'm on their staff."

"Sounds like plain old politics to me. What happened to all your scruples?"

"It's just...I get tired of all our friends and relatives offering to loan us money. I'm the only one that went to college. I have two degrees, but they are all better paid than I am. They get commissions, bonus money, and all kinds of incentive pay. Perhaps now with a crack at merit pay...Anyway, you have to blow your own horn. The squeaky wheel gets the grease. It isn't what you know, it's who you..."

"Oh, knock it off, will you?"

Saturday night arrived and our little Nash Rambler was humming along like a sewing machine. The sound of music was floating from the gym as I turned into the parking lot. What luck! Two school board members were parking their cars, and there was room between them for my own. Driving expertly, I wheeled in between the green Cadillac and blue Lincoln. Mud and water flew into the air.

"Good show!" Dorothy cried. "You got both cars. It isn't easy to splash two at the same time."

Doctor X seemed quite upset about the whole thing. I hurried to get out of the car. When I opened my door, the wind banged it against the side of Doctor Y's car.

"I'm sorry," I apologized.

"Sorry for what?" he growled. "For not breaking the window, too?"

Never missing an opportunity to encourage her husband, my wife whispered, "Attaboy, sport. That's letting 'em know who you are."

Inside the gym, a few smiling ladies had coerced their escorts onto the dance floor. The remaining non-combatants had formed small groups to shout small talk above the din. The decorating committee had adopted the theme of a Paris sidewalk café, but the décor came off more like Ed's Carry-Out Pizza.

I spied Doctor X conversing with Doctor Y. I moved in on them. Doctor X was saying that he had just given his 16-year-old son a Jaguar, an airplane, and karate lessons for which he flies to Minneapolis.

I boasted, "My son has a Honda 90 trail bike."

He answered, "How nice." I kissed his hand.

Doctor Y casually mentioned that he had recently bought a 30-foot houseboat to use strictly on the river. He also bought a red upholstered Cris-Craft complete with bar for walleye fishing on the lakes.

I blurted, "I have a plywood duck boat. It fits right on top of my car."

Having impressed Doctors X and Y, I glanced around for other school board members. Aha! There was Doctor Z the middle of a large gathering. I melted quietly into the group. The topic of conversation was travel. Apparently everyone had just returned from Hawaii or the Bahamas, or was leaving for Europe or Sun Valley. Doctor Z was saying, "We certainly enjoy the slopes at Aspen this time of year."

I interjected, "My superintendent let me go 30 miles to Springview for an ACT workshop. Of course, I had to take two nuns from the parochial high school along with me. The school paid me seven cents a mile and bought my lunch too. Golly, that was really living."

Doctor Z peered intently at me. "I like your attitude, Son. What's your name?"

"Wayne Barham, sir, and this is my wife, Dorothy." We bowed and curtsied and backed onto the dance floor, disappearing among the mass calisthenics. It was a grand exit. Only Spencer Tracy and Katharine Hepburn could have pulled it off better.

I led Dort off the other side of the dance floor and into the spectators. "That was a quick dance," she complained. But I had other board members to stalk.

Jackpot! There sat Mr. Davis, with his wife, at a corner table. He was the richest man in town. He was also the biggest bore. We accidentally strode directly to their table. They invited us to join them. He was eager to relate his success story to anyone who would listen. He began by informing me of his financial wizardry, then gave me a thump on the back and said, "I started out as a teacher just like you."

"I didn't know that," I encouraged.

"I've wished a thousand times I had never quit teaching," he lied. It's a noble profession. But I quit teaching and started to peddle books to schools. It was tough, but I clawed and scratched my way to the vice-presidency of the company." (Married the president's daughter and retired, a millionaire, at 54.) He let me know that, even though retired, he still managed to turn a shrewd deal or two.

I looked him straight in the eye and said, "I had a $100 war bond once, but I cashed it in when I got married."

Mrs. Davis turned to Dorothy and said, "That's a very pretty dress."

Dort smiled, "Thank you."

I pressed on, "She made it herself. And she bakes bread and makes homemade sauerkraut in a real crock."

"My," Mrs. Davis answered, "that sounds delicious. Our present cook has been a disappointment. We have had dreadful luck with servants lately. It is so difficult to get competent help these days."

I could see she was green with envy. My parting shot was, "Dorothy knows more than 50 different ways to use hamburger in recipes. And she cans pickles!"

"How quaint," she gasped.

The band's vocalist was singing, "Two different worlds...we live in two different worlds..."

Dort tugged at my arm and dragged me away to the punch bowl. I could see she was miffed. "What's the matter with you?" I asked.

She answered through clenched teeth. "Where is your pride? What happened to the man I married? It's not like you to grovel. Is merit pay that important to you?"

"I've gone this far and I'm not going to blow it now. I only have three more board members to butter up. All three of them right over there. I can get the whole covey with one shot. Trust me."

The covey included Harry Jones, the local banker, Lars Johnson, president of the Savings and Loan, and Ole Olson of Olson's Insurance. The banker was relating his favorite golf story. Last summer he had played in a foursome including Olson, Johnson, and Doctor X. As Jones leaned over his ball for an eight-foot-putt, Doctor X said, "Five hundred dollars says you miss, Harry."

The banker didn't hesitate. "You're on, sport."

I gulped at the thought of my entire month's salary riding on a single putt. As the story continued, Harry missed the putt. He paid off the $500 over a martini in the clubhouse bar. I recalled borrowing $150 from this same man's bank to pay for my son's tonsillectomy (by Doctor X).

Several people were still laughing and joshing Jones about dropping the $500 when I heard my own voice saying, "When I was a small boy I was a caddy. I still remember that the richest men invariably owned the heaviest golf bags and tipped the least." I was rambling. "I won the World Series pool once. They held it in the barbershop and it was worth five bucks. I was so happy and excited I nearly wet my pants."

A deafening silence followed. Ole Olson broke it by clearing his throat. He ventured, "Uh, I took a trip up North recently and bagged a polar bear. My guide spotted him from the air. He couldn't escape, because there was no place to hide. We chased him around in circles until he was exhausted. Then we landed the plane, and I walked right up to him. It only took one shot. Let me tell you, it was great sport."

"I'll bet the bear loved it," I muttered.

Ignoring me, he continued. I learned that his trip, including the outfitter's fee, cost more than my entire yearly salary. He looked at me and said, "I've heard that you really love the outdoors. Why haven't you gone after a polar bear, Wayne?"

"In the first place, shooting an animal under the conditions you just described makes me sick to my stomach. And secondly, my old man couldn't afford to set me up in the insurance business," I snarled.

Mr. Johnson intervened, "Look here, Son. You're implying that you might be underpaid? I want you to know that we are raising the base pay of our teachers all the way up to $6,400 for next year. Now I feel that this is most generous. As we see it, a family of four should live quite comfortably on $6,400, if they are careful. Money is scarce. Even the president says we must tighten our belts. We simply have to draw the line somewhere."

"Maybe we have been reckless with our money and haven't budgeted wisely. Why just recently the president himself was raised a paltry $100,000. And the senators limited their increases to a mere $12,000 per year. Now that's what I call self-sacrifice. I guess it is my patriotic duty to fight inflation too."

My sarcasm was wasted. Mr. Johnson beamed. "That's the spirit, young man. Now then, did I tell you fellows that my wife and I plan to camp in Europe this summer? No guided tours and rushing around for us! We are buying a new camper, one of those self-propelled jobs. Man, it's a regular home on wheels. I got a few drinks into old Ed over at Smith Motors and he finally pushed that pencil down to 13,000 bucks. We're going to take our sweet old time and spend the whole summer camping in Europe. That's the only way to go, right? Where would you suggest we go first?"

I savored each word and I spoke slowly and distinctly. "You can go straight to hell, and take the other six philanthropists on this school board with you."

I had just committed professional hara-kiri. It felt great.

Upon my arrival at school on Monday morning I was summoned to the superintendent's office. I had never visited the inner sanctum before. I should have known that a man making $25,000 would have an impressive office, but this took my breath away. I felt an urge to take off my shoes and feel the plush carpet with my bare feet. He was putting across the floor into an electric ball-return. I mentally compared his office with my classroom. Would it be poor timing to ask if the crack in my chalkboard could be repaired?

He leaned his putter against the wall and stared at me in obvious disbelief before mumbling, "Australia is accepting applications from American teachers. Have you ever thought of...?"

I climbed the stairs and entered my classroom just as the last bell was ringing. The principal's voice was droning the usual announcements via the squawk box. He ended on a personal note to the faculty. "You are reminded that next year's requisitions for supplies are due in my office today. The school board has suggested that you cut your lists to a bare minimum in order to save money. Paper clips, chalk, and thumbtacks must be used with discretion. I trust you will cooperate in this matter. Please remember to turn off your classroom lights when you leave for your lunch break."

PART FIVE

Counseling Experience

I was a counselor at Mitchell High School in South Dakota for two years, 1965-1967. During this time, "The Sound of Music" was a big hit. Malcolm X, the Black Muslim leader, was assassinated. Martin Luther King held the march from Selma to Montgomery. Ralph Nader, a young lawyer, was a leader in the fight for new safety regulations, since a record 52,500 Americans had died, and 9,000,000 were injured in car accidents in 1966. General Motors hired investigators to question Nader's friends and neighbors. The Green Bay Packers beat the Kansas City Chiefs 35-10 in the first Superbowl. Huge marches in New York City and San Francisco protested the Vietnam War. Race riots in Detroit killed 40 people. These were violent times.

There were two basic theories of counseling. One concept was to give direct advice, and the other was to follow Roger's idea of letting the client work through his own problems. A typical Rogers technique was to get the person to talk and then if a lull in the conversation came up, the counselor would simply repeat what the client had said last. Like, "You feel then that...?"

At any rate, I soon found myself sort of like a wishy-washy Charlie Brown. I became a middle-of-the-road eclectic. It took me awhile to realize I was being lied to. I tried to sort through sincere tears and the crocodile tears of hypocrisy.

It didn't take long to discover that most kids came to me because they had no one else that would listen. Sometimes I never said a word, just listened. After a 15- or 20-minute tirade by a kid, he or she would suddenly stand up and say, "Thank you so much. I feel so much better." I hadn't done a thing. This wasn't restricted to the students. Teachers would drop in just to "chat" but soon spilled their guts to unburden themselves. I believe it was because they didn't want to whine to a spouse, or didn't feel comfortable talking to an administrator, or didn't trust their peers, so it came down to confidentiality. There are a lot of lonely people out there. Loneliness or boredom is the most deadly killer of man.

In my opinion, unhappy, intact homes are more productive of delinquency than broken homes. I can easily accept the fact that 50% of all hospital beds in America are filled with mental patients.

It didn't take me long to discover which teachers the students flocked to and those they wished to avoid. I heard comments like:

"The only thing our math teacher teaches us is how to be a zero."

"Our English teacher can make a simple sentence seem complex."

"He makes us feel important."

"What we think makes a difference in her class."

The personal characteristics of good teachers are enthusiasm, energy, openness, concern, imagination, and being in possession of a good sense of humor.

Bad teaching is associated with stupidity, arrogance, narrowness, cynicism, dullness, insensitivity, and corrosive sarcasm. The psychology of learning has escaped these people. They will never learn to minimize deficiencies and at the same time neutralize rage.

Teenagers can be candid at times. Peggy comes into my office and immediately states, "I get along fine with my stepmother. It's my father I can't stand." She shifts gears and says, "My girlfriends don't like me because I'm a whore."

"Do they call you a whore?"

"No."

"Then how do you know they feel this way about you?"

"Because I am a whore."

"Oh!"

A senior boy says, "I'm having a problem with my dad."

What sort of problem?"

"I want to go to a private college, but he thinks it's too spendy. He has all kinds of money. He can afford it."

"So?"

"So, I have a friend already in school there, and Dad agreed to drive down there with me to look the school over. My friend's roommate sleeps on the floor and the only furniture in their room is a tree stump for a table and a refrigerator full of beer. Dad says I'm not going to school there."

"I see."

"I told him I know about the woman he has been fooling around with these past months, and I wondered if Mom might like to know."

"That's blackmail. You wouldn't blackmail your father, would you?"

"Hey, whose side are you on?"

"I'm not taking sides with anyone."

He gets up to leave and I ask, "Let me know how this comes out?"

"You really want to know?"

"Sure."

"Do you get your jollies by listening to this kind of stuff?"

"Not really. It's part of my job. Let's talk again."

Another student is sent to me by a teacher. Marvin has been in lots of trouble with the police. Minor stuff but numerous encounters. The judge puts him on probation and sentenced him to stay in school. The probation failed to stipulate that he attend regularly and put forth an honest effort to pass. He has failed everything for the past two years.

"Marvin, don't you get tired of being sent here to talk to me?"

"No, you're a nice guy."

"Thanks, but why don't you ask the judge if you can quit? This isn't working out at all. Marvin, you're 19 years old."

"I like it here."

Two girls are cutting their hair in the restroom. They forget to eat lunch during their assigned lunch hour. Now they belong in the study hall but want to eat. One of the girls says, "I feel faint when I don't eat."

I'm having a bad day. "Okay, go to the study hall and faint." I can count on an irate phone call from her mother tonight.

Another day. Steve was sentenced to 10 days in jail for driving around the school and tearing up the lawn. He also used a nail to scratch the ceramic tile along the wall of an entire corridor of our new school. He is slouched in a chair, glaring at me.

"What's wrong, Steve?"

"I hate my mother." Pause.

"So, you hate your mother?"

"I didn't ask to be adopted, you know. My dad ain't my real dad, either."

You don't like him?"

"I don't like anyone." Pause.

"You surely must like someone?"

"I used to like my dog."

"Used to?"

"Yeah. I had a stuffed toy giraffe, see? I came home two days ago and my dog had chewed it to pieces. I kicked and stomped him. Beat the hell out of him. He took off and I haven't seen him since. Now tell me, if you can't trust your own dog, who can you trust?"

The next day, Steve stopped me in the hallway and said his dog came home. Sad.

James was a soft-spoken, well-mannered honor student. He closed the door behind him and began to nervously pace the floor. Reminded me of a coyote in a zoo. "I can't sleep nights. Can you get me some sleeping pills?"

"No, I can't do that. You should talk to your parents or your doctor."

"I can't do that." Then out of left field, he blurts, "I'm doing terrible things. I bury live chickens up to their necks and then throw rocks at their heads. I put little firecrackers, you know—ladyfingers—down frogs' throats, light 'em and see how many hops they make before they explode. I go into the barn at night with a flashlight and catch birds. I staple their little feet to the floor and put jar lids of food and water in front of them just out of reach. Sometimes they live quite awhile."

"Why are you telling me all this?"

"Because I know you won't tell anyone."

"We have a psychiatrist that visits our school every Thursday afternoon. I want you to see him and tell him what you have told me. He will help you, James."

"You know they are still looking for the guy that switched all those tombstones in the cemetery? I did it."

"Tell all this to Dr. Evander. Then maybe you can sleep." I felt like a priest at confession. What is truly confidential? At what point do you confide in someone else? Who do you tell?

I don't know who designed the typing rooms. They are two fairly small adjoining rooms separated by a glass see-through partition. A door can be opened or closed between them. At times, this could allow two classes to be held at the same time. Danny tells me, "I admit I screwed up, and I told Mr. Bauer I was sorry. He told me I had to sit alone in that other typing room until he said I could come back into the room with the rest of the class."

I didn't ask if the crime had been ruled a misdemeanor or a felony. Danny continued, "I can barely hear what goes on in the other room, and I can't read what's on the board at all. I'd like to move back with the rest of the class. I feel like I've got a contagious disease."

I smiled, "That doesn't seem too severe to me, Dan. How long have you been banished to the other room?"

"Two months."

"Two months?" I thundered. "Thanks for coming in, Dan."

I checked Bauer's schedule and found he had a free or planning period 3rd period. He was sitting at his desk, alone as always, when I walked into his room. "Dan tells me he has been ostracized from your class for two months. I think this is a bit much."

"This is my class. Who do you think you are? I'm teaching him a lesson in obedience. I'm busy, so if you don't mind?"

I held my temper and surprised myself with my low-key tone of voice. "Perhaps I should set up a conference with you, Dan's mother, our principal, and even Mr. McCardle, the superintendent. I'm sure that when all the facts come out, this can be settled amiably." God I was proud of myself as I turned and walked away from this weasel.

That same day, Dan told me, "Guess what? Mr. Bauer let me come back with the rest of the kids. Neat, huh?"

One of the rewarding moments of my life. It warmed the cockles of me Irish heart.

It is January. School has just resumed after a nice pleasant and needed Christmas vacation. Two boys, not noted for their academic achievement, were waiting for me at 7:45 a.m. I unlocked my door, "What brings you guys here so early this morning?"

It took me awhile to understand what they were saying, as they both spoke at once. Themes were due in their senior English class. As usual, they had procrastinated but decided to knock out their themes during Christmas vacation. They figured they might even earn brownie points by being the first to hand in their work. They even located and used the public library for research. So they went that extra mile and took their papers to Mr. Adams' home before New Year's Day. They couldn't wait to see the smile on his face when they surprised him. Wrong. Without looking at their work, he caustically and unemotionally stated, "Bill, I told you to fold your paper lengthwise with the fold on the right. You put the fold on the left. And Ray, you were told to put English 4 at the top of the folded paper, then your name, and then the date. You put your name first. Following directions is far more important than the content of your work. I should throw these into the wastebasket, but I will accept and read them. But whatever letter grade you receive will be marked down a grade for not doing as you were told."

School boards have the authority to accept or ban books from their libraries. Some of the books that have been banned in the United States are *The Godfather*, *Airport*, *Summer of '42*, *The Naked Ape*, *The Learning Tree*, *Catcher in the Rye*, *Bury My Heart at Wounded Knee*, and *Psychology Today* magazine.

Catcher in the Rye was banned from Mitchell High School's library. That summer, we were visiting friends in Wisconsin. Their teenaged daughter was reading *Catcher*. I told her that the book she was reading was banned from our school library in South Dakota. "Really? My English teacher gave us a list of five books to read this summer. This is one of them." A book banned in one school is required reading in another.

In one town, the book *Girls & Sex* was banned from the sex education classes, while *Boys & Sex* was not. *Bury My Heart at Wounded Knee* was banned in one school, because it was branded un-American by an administrator. While visiting in my hometown, Champaign, Illinois, I got out a phone book and dialed the number of Dee Brown, the author of the Wounded Knee book. I asked if I could bring my copy of his book to his house in Urbana to be signed. He said he would be happy to oblige. My wife and I found him to be a very gracious and modest person. During our conversation, I mentioned that I was sure his students were a big help in doing research for him. A shriek came from the kitchen. His wife appeared in the doorway, "On the contrary, he is such a soft touch, he helps his students with their research." At any rate, we agreed that words are neither good nor bad, only thinking makes them so.

Two years a counselor in a large high school provided me a unique opportunity. I was presented a seat that afforded a hard look at the broad spectrum of education. The scene from the counselor's office is probably the most impartial, unbiased, and objective view that can be had. I was involved in everything that happened, and yet, I could sit back and observe with an open mind. I was neither teacher, student, parent, custodian, board member, coach, nor superintendent. I was more like God, sitting there watching the whole scene unfold day after day. After awhile I began to feel like a sexless inanimate object. I was in the middle of the action, but I was mostly a listening post, everyone's friend, and a neutral "King's X" in the middle of a perpetual battleground.

A high school compares favorably with a never-ending Broadway play. New faces move across the stage, but emotions remain the same year after year. People of each generation experience the same old feelings. Frustration, anger, fear, hate, tears, tragedy, joy, laughter, and love are intertwined like vines growing randomly through the trees of a forest.

It was like being inside a huge squirrel cage. Everyone was on a treadmill. The students were running toward graduation, while the teachers counted the days until vacation.

Counselors usually feel that they are pawns to be moved around as stopgaps by administrators. They are asked to fill in as substitute teachers when coaches leave early on trips or when any teacher becomes ill. They are left to run the ship when the principal is out of town on various "business" trips. Generally speaking, counselors sometimes end up catching the unpleasant duties that the administrators should be doing themselves.

It was in the room marked "Counselor" that I really became empathetic toward students. Complaints and problems involving teachers came out of the same rooms each day. Conversely, other teachers received nothing but praise. I soon found that the students all wanted to be in a handful of teachers' rooms and they all tried to avoid certain teachers. This was no different than the college scene, except in college the students work out their schedules to include the good and avoid the bad. The high school kid is stuck with the wheel of fortune. Administrators refuse to admit they have any bad teachers, so the parents and students are informed that they will have no choice of teachers. In fact, computerized scheduling resolves this problem in the larger high schools.

As a counselor, let's suppose I was asked to work out the schedules for two new students. I could assign four bad teachers to one of them while giving four good teachers to the other. The result would be like day and night. One student would be miserable, frustrated, unhappy and cheated. The other would be motivated, happy, and well educated. In other words, teachers are the key to the entire educational picture.

Administrators are only whistling in the dark when they won't admit they have poor teachers on their staffs. I don't advocate allowing students the power to hire and fire teachers. However, we are sadly missing the boat by not giving them the privilege of rating teachers. The good teachers wouldn't mind at all. The overwhelming majority of teachers are against it because there are so many poor ones, and they fear for their jobs. They rationalize that the kids are too young, they will make teaching a popularity contest, and teachers will all start giving high marks to please the students. Balderdash!! The students know good teaching when they are exposed to it, and I'll put my money on them when it comes to honesty in rating. Only recently has quantity in teaching been reached. I feel that student rating of teachers would be a giant step forward in upgrading the quality of teaching.

Most administrators force the counselor to keep a myriad of records to prove the worth of his position to the school board and visiting accrediting teams. A sound program of guidance must devote time for counseling on a person-to-person basis. Counselors are up to their necks in stuffing the files with countless papers and forms to impress the higher-ups in the educational hierarchy.

There are teachers that take points off test scores for misspelled words. For example, a boy came to me and said, "Mr. X gave us a test in history and I got 49 out of 50 right on the test. That should have been a 98. Right? By the time he got through taking off for spelling, I got a C-. I really studied for that test, but I've always been a lousy speller. That's not fair. Is he teaching history or spelling?"

A boy in industrial arts, music, or art can be penalized the same way by being a poor speller on tests. Personally, I couldn't care less whether or not the mechanic who works on my car can spell. The same goes for my TV repairman or my dentist.

Administrators who claim this gives an added hour to the school day for increased curriculum justify the closed noon hour. Translated it means the parents don't want the kids to come home for lunch, because most parents are working. It also means that the police don't want the kids in their cars, and the businessmen don't want them downtown. The result is a 25-minute lunch hour with most of it spent standing in line. No wonder more and more young people are developing ulcers. They must bolt their food like animals to make it to their next class on time. This is also the only time all day long that the kids have time to talk to their friends and relax. The rest of the time is spent in classes and study hall where no talking is permitted. Even teachers get a free period to drink coffee, and relax. The students are nearly stir-crazy by the time that last bell rings. They can hardly wait to break out just to exercise and talk.

The study hall is the greatest single curse on the high school scene. The teacher in charge usually makes more noise yelling for silence than the students who are whispering. In most cases, personal letters cannot be read nor written. I have seen teachers snatch personal letters from students and read them. This is very unfair and an invasion of privacy. I would think that letter writing should be encouraged in the study halls, but it is usually considered a cardinal sin.

A high school principal was approached by a student council member as to the possibility of piping soft background music into the study hall through the P.A. system. The student's reasoning was that the kids usually study by music at home and it would cover the hum or buzzing that sometimes prevails in the study hall. The principal answered, "Why don't we bring in the Shrine Circus and parade the elephants through there if you must be entertained. This is a school, not a dance hall!"

Sometimes kids are packed into auditoriums or cafeterias that double for study halls. Two or three hundred high school kids can really give a teacher a bad time if they choose. I'm surprised that they are as well behaved as they are. Sitting elbow to elbow in cramped quarters and playing kneesies under the table is not conducive to quiet and perfect conduct. It is especially difficult when you are seventeen and bursting with energy.

An administrator displayed the epitome in ignorance during the week of final exams. It was the very last day of school. All books had been checked in, no assignments were given, thus no homework, and the library was closed. All students who didn't have an exam were still required to sit in the study hall anyway. They furthermore were forced to sit quietly, no talking, hands folded on desks, and no sleeping. There was absolutely no reason for those kids to be in school. What a way to remember all summer your last two hours in school! Is it any wonder that kids hate school? I'm surprised they didn't tell that individual to go to hell and walk out en masse.

The library should be the hub of the school. It should be the most important part of the school. Instead, it often times is sorely inadequate, sadly managed, and seldom used. It becomes the most difficult place to reach in the school. Students usually need a pink slip from a teacher stating a specific assignment or they are not admitted. Students are turned away nearly every period because they don't have a pink slip or there isn't room for them.

We build our gyms with seating for thousands, and our libraries sometimes won't accommodate 15 people.

Librarians seem to be handpicked people who love books but hate students. The general rule is to discourage kids through red tape and plain old bureaucracy to the point of giving up hope of ever reaching the library. It is easier to get tickets to a Broadway play than gain admittance to some high school libraries. If admittance is finally achieved into the inner sanctum, the student is made to feel that it is okay to look, but don't touch!

I visited a school where the day was divided into 45-minute periods. The librarian admitted students by appointment only. The first 10 minutes was spent in roll taking and the collecting of pink slips. She also enforced a rule that demanded all books and periodicals be returned to the shelves 15 minutes before the final bell at the close of the period. This left 20 minutes to use the library, and no browsing was tolerated.

High school kids are pathetically eager to talk to someone in the schools about their problems. A few teachers are blessed with a genuine concern for their students. These teachers have verified a common complaint of the students: "The teachers don't really care about me as a person, and they make me feel as though I'm imposing on them if I ask for extra help. I'm afraid to go in before or after school because he will chew me out. He might find out how dumb I really am. Then too, the kids might see me and call me a brownnoser."

This is where I was introduced to the real importance of peer group learning. I was told that I was to be the National Honor Society advisor. During our first meeting it became obvious that our main function was to sponsor the spring ceremony involving the induction of new members. This also entailed giving a tea for the parents. After having been an old coach for the past fifteen years, with the smell of the locker room still in my nostrils, a National Honor Society tea was a new experience. It was evident that this one ceremony was the "biggie" for the year. This was it; yellow roses, silver service set, punch and cookies, napkins, and nut cups to be arranged on special tablecloths.

The fifteen or twenty members of the organization represented the cream of the crop, academically speaking, from our entire school. The whole bit seemed like a waste of brainpower. I asked the members if they might be interested in offering a free tutoring service. Their response was overwhelming. I was bowled over by their enthusiasm. We decided to offer our services before and after school and during study hall time. These kids turned out to be the most unselfish people I've ever had the pleasure of knowing.

The weekly failing list was one of my responsibilities, so a list of eligible students needing our services was readily available. The next step was to interview kids experiencing trouble in various subjects. Again I was astounded by their response. As in the case of each member of my prospective tutoring service, not one of the kids needing help refused aid. I began matching tutors with failing students, and we soon had four or five kids assigned to each tutor.

The results were nearly instantaneous and very rewarding. It was warming to see them operate like old hens with baby chicks. They developed a rapport that was missing in most student-teacher relationships. The threat of embarrassment in class, the traumatic feeling of shame, ridicule, and scorn was removed. There developed from these sessions some counseling, advice giving, encouragement, and praise. These were by-products, but they were the necessary ingredients missing from the classrooms. Like forgetting to add the subtle nuance of cinnamon or nutmeg to a fresh apple pie.

The tutors gave of themselves unselfishly. They developed competition to see who could get their people off the failing list the fastest. The students were tremendously enthusiastic about this new project, and the parents called and thanked us repeatedly. Everyone was pleased and thrilled except, guess who? Some of the teachers themselves. They took this as a personal affront. They grumbled things such as, "The counselor's grandstand play. All they do is louse up those dumb kids. If we can't teach them, how is some snot-nosed kid going to do it? They will never learn to think on their own. I wish I'd had someone to do all my homework for me in high school," etc.

All I can say is that the failing kids volunteered to go unashamedly and eagerly to the tutors for extra help. Here was peer group learning at its best. Somewhere along the line, the doors of communication had been shut between the students and teachers. The icy snows of pessimism and cynicism had broken the lines.

There are some school policies that are not clear to me. For instance, a normal class load for the average student is four plus phys ed. and/or band. A better than average student can petition for five classes if his grades show that he can handle the extra class. Then how about the student who has failed several courses and is behind in credits? Oftentimes he is given six classes so that he might catch up. In the past he couldn't handle four so we give him six!

Most schools conduct elaborate political campaigns each fall prior to electing class officers. Usually the only group that holds any meetings is the junior class, which is stuck with financing the spring prom. I asked a principal why all the officers were elected if no meetings were held. He replied, "We have to fill up the yearbook with something, don't we?"

The same could be said about most student councils. The principal gives his yearly inspirational speech, which emphasizes the importance of student government. He then proceeds to postpone or cancel the meetings or veto all suggestions made by the student leaders. General apathy sets in after awhile. No problems, no waves.

A common punishment is the three-day suspension from school. This can be won by a variety of felonies including insubordination, smoking in the john, and truancy. The sentence usually carries the customary zeroes while they are gone. If the object is to make students aware of the importance of attendance, does it make sense to suspend them for three days? That's like the irate father spanking his seven-year-old son while saying, "I'll teach you to beat up on your smaller brother!"

One of the most highly competitive games played is called "catch the bastards smoking in the john." The smell of smoke is in the air all the time, so the rules say the principal must catch the boy with the cigarette in his hand. The more experienced veterans will operate in pairs. One serves as a lookout while the other sits on the stool and smokes. If the partner in crime flashes a prearranged signal to his cohort he quickly flushes the cigarette down the stool. The object of the game is for the principal to dispatch the sentry and catch the guilty culprit with his pants down around his ankles. The ensuing three-day suspension usually "makes" the day for the battle-hardened principal. It is a well-deserved trophy for the hunter over the hunted. I'm a bit vague as to why it requires a master's degree to play the part of the hunter. Which advanced course covers this type of game in graduate school?

Most student failure is really teacher failure. A secondary school with a faculty of 50 will be fortunate to include 5 or 10 outstanding teachers. There are many incompetent teachers in our schools. Some are actually proud of being "tough" and sometimes boast of how many students they fail. One man bragged that he had flunked all but three kids on a semester test. I suggested that perhaps the test was too hard and grading on a curve might have been a solution. He sneered, "Are you kidding?" It was evident he received his jollies by the number of kids he could flunk.

Schools are places where students learn to be stupid. Memorization and conformity are duly rewarded. The creative child that thinks ideas instead of things is censured.

Tenure protects the poor teacher. He rides along year after year on the salary schedule. How many occupations are there where a man is protected by tenure when he is inadequate and doesn't produce? It seems the poor ones stay in teaching and good ones go into other fields after a few years.

Teachers become apathetic and lethargic because of the automatic salary schedules. This takes away incentive. Merit pay would be a step in the right direction, but the teachers themselves fight it. That's because there are more poor teachers than outstanding ones. The longer you teach the more you notice the poor teacher receiving the same salary as the good one. He never volunteers for anything. He is the last teacher to arrive in the morning, and the first to leave in the afternoon. He never attempts to read or keep up on the latest trends in education, and he is never asked to sponsor any organizations. Students never come to his room before or after school for extra help, and everyone treats him as though he has leprosy. Nevertheless, through tenure he rises to the top step of the salary schedule. He has reached his level of inadequacy, and hundreds of suffering students are his byproduct.

I've had administrators tell me in confidence, "Wayne, I would love to get rid of Mr. R, and hire your young student teacher. He really is great, and the kids love him."

"Then why don't you?"

He then explains, "Mr. R. has been here a long time and is nearing retirement, and I wouldn't dare. Everyone has hated him for 25 years, so I suppose we can stand him for a few more."

I cringe in my seat and die a little inside each time I watch a poor teacher in action. I've heard experienced teachers commit the most glaring grammatical errors. They say things such as, "I seen, he done, or I'm going to learn you how to do it."

There are teachers with chronic bad breath and others with B.O. that would stop a train. I actually saw salt rings under the armpits of a teacher's jacket, and I'm certain that coat had never seen a cleaning establishment. I couldn't stand it in the same room, so I left. The students remained a captive audience. That's really bad.

There is no doubt that there are many power-seekers in teaching. There are some bitter men and women whose sole purpose in life seems to be that of making young people miserable. There are some who even approach sadism. They feel that child must suffer to learn, and there can't be any real learning taking place if the students are enjoying themselves.

There are homosexuals, perverts, and alcoholics teaching in our schools. The strange thing is that these people never seem to be fired. They usually are allowed to resign, and then they move on to another town. Why are they allowed to continue in teaching? Don't make waves.

Teachers miss the boat by not taking advantage of peer group learning. Most of them believe that if the teacher isn't talking there is no learning taking place. In fact, interaction is a word that is unfamiliar to most teachers. They are excellent talkers but very poor listeners. Professional speakers claim that the poorest and most ill mannered audience to address is a large group of teachers. Observe them at a teachers' convention, and you will readily see how rude they are to a speaker. Yet they demand the undivided attention of their students.

Most discipline problems stem from the school, the teacher, the home, and the student in that order. The schools set forth far too many rules, dumb regulations, and outdated policies. The teachers compound these mistakes with punitive teaching methods and unfair forms of punishment. Kids don't enroll in our high schools; they are incarcerated.

Teachers make the mistake of underestimating an individual's worth. To be humiliated in front of the peer group is the most devastating thing that can happen to a student. When he loses his pride and dignity he is stripped and standing naked. Even a rabbit or a mouse will stand and fight when cornered. Teachers make remarks such as, "If you don't like it, you can just get up and leave." The student feels challenged and sometimes leaves in spite of the consequences. Another common remark is, "You really think you are funny, don't you?" The student usually feels he must make a sarcastic rebuttal to save face. In other words, most barbed remarks and sarcasm are initiated and brought about by the teacher. In most cases, the student is merely protecting his image.

A good example of this took place in an industrial arts class. A boy completed a small project in woodworking class but had failed to start another project. The teacher told the boy to bring the materials for another project and get busy. He was unaware that the boy was very poor and couldn't afford to buy the material. The boy was ashamed to admit that his family was so poor, so he started goofing around in the shop because of his idleness. This angered the teacher and he lost his temper and shouted at the already ashamed boy, "If you don't like this class, get the hell out of here."

Seeing a way out of an uncomfortable situation in front of his friends, the boy left. The word soon spread to the other faculty members that he was a troublemaker and was to be watched carefully.

Time shows that an unjust society or situation cannot endure, because those outside its benefit will revolt. Vandalism involving schools has always been a common occurrence. Why have the schools been such a popular target for obvious hostility? Kids see the building as a symbol of all their frustrations and pent-up emotions. They attack the school because they don't dare defend themselves verbally or physically against the teachers. Other students eventually turn the school off and tune the teachers out.

They become remarkably adept at staring intently at the teacher, reacting with varied facial expressions, while daydreaming in another world.

Students drop out of school due to repeated failure or discontent due to unhappiness and a lack of interest. Teachers should bring more realistic experiences into the classroom to supplement textbooks. Information would become more interesting and meaningful. Experience usually improves and broadens a teacher, but unfortunately, some teachers only wear the rut of boredom and mediocrity deep with each passing year. They fail to keep up with the times by traveling, reading, exchanging ideas, and varying their methods and techniques.

Teachers have a way of talking to their students instead of talking with them. This closes the door to spontaneous discussion of ideas. Most students eventually give up in despair and resign themselves to listening to their teacher's views on everything. Many interesting topics involve no right or wrong responses, but the student is afraid to express his own feelings, opinions, and ideas if they conflict with the obvious philosophy of the teacher. Students slant their themes and term papers for the same reason. They are writing what the instructor wants to read, and not what the student really wants to write. Ask any student. It's a can of worms.

Learning is more important than teaching. Schools are for the students, not the teachers. Teachers facetiously quote the cliché, "This would be a darn good job if it weren't for the students." Unfortunately, there are those who believe it.

A typical class with the traditional teacher goes something like this:

Scene: Mr. Johnson's government class. Johnson is the stereotype of the traditional secondary teacher. White shirt, bowtie, cuffed pants three inches above shoe tops, white sox, crew-cut hair with no sideburns, trace of shaving cream behind one ear. A tyrant in class, straight lecture right from the book, squelches any attempt at spontaneous discussion from class, usually derives pleasure from calling on students who do not raise hands.

Students are well disciplined. They arrive on time and are in seats before bell rings. One boy is just sitting down as bell rings:

Mr. Johnson: "Earl, you weren't in your seat before the bell rang. Go to the office for a tardy slip. Don't come back without a pink slip." Looks at grade book, "Edna and Alice were gone yesterday. Let me see your pink attendance slips."

Formal rules and regulations taken care of. "This being Friday, I have decided to try something different in class today. I have been accused of being a narrow-minded teacher. Never mind by whom. Today, anything goes. The book is closed, and you can discuss anything that you care to bring up and I promise to keep an open mind. Feel free to say anything you like and I will listen to your ideas. After all, you are the leaders of tomorrow. Who will start?"

Frank: "Is it true that we have quite a problem with homosexuality in our prisons, but no one ever wants to talk about it?"

Mr. Johnson: "I'm sure we can think of more pleasant subjects to discuss. Besides there are girls present."

Mary: "Are there really tax dodges for the rich while the salaried have to pay their share?"

Mr. Johnson: "I'm certain all Americans feel an obligation to pay their taxes."

Tom: "I read where organized crime skims off the top 10% of our national income. I also heard that the money that goes to organized crime matches the income of our six largest corporations."

Mr. Johnson: "Figures lie and liars figure. I think those things get blown out of proportion."

Tom again: "The word is that the school board plans to cut out all the 'frills' in our school next year because of lack of money. That will include phys ed. And drivers' training. We have far more people killed on the highways than in wars and yet they take away drivers' education?"

Mary: "We have hungry people right here in our country. Our school doesn't have enough money for drivers' ed. And physical education. How we can we justify spending billions of dollars on space programs and such an unpopular war in Vietnam?"

Mr. Johnson: "I'm sure our president will guide us in the right direction."

Ed: "Sure, you can say that, but we young guys have to fight the dumb war. Old soldiers never die. Young ones do."

Mr. Johnson: "Now look here. I'm a veteran of World War II, the Big War. (Three years working in the PX at Chanute Field with weekends spent chasing girls in nearby Chicago.)

Ed: "Let's take a vote on how we feel about the war. Those who think we should be in Viet Nam raise your hand...six? All against? Twenty-four. There's your answer."

Mr. Johnson: "I didn't authorize that vote. If the principal hears about this, just remember it wasn't my idea."

Bill: "May I please go to the bathroom?"

Mr. Johnson: "Did you have to interrupt the class for that?"

Bill: "Well I have to have a pink slip, don't I? It's rather ridiculous. I'll be nineteen when I graduate and I'll have to go fight in a war I don't believe in. I have to ask permission for a pink slip to go to the bathroom. Where but school do you have to have permission to go to the bathroom? You know something else? I can get married, but I can't buy a drink on my honeymoon. (Applause from class.)

Mr. Johnson: (Whines) "I don't make the rules, but it's my job to enforce them. Someone change the subject."

Diane: "My parents planned to build a small new home this summer but when the interest rates on loans were raised, they felt they just couldn't afford it. If the banks and loan companies have all the money anyway, why raise the interest rates at a time when we face a severe housing shortage? I read where the construction of new homes fell off 26% last month."

Mr. Johnson: I don't understand your attitude, Diane. You make it sound as if the rich get richer and the poor get poorer. (Voice gets loud and high-pitched.) I'll tell you one thing. This is my country, right or wrong. (Bangs fist on desk.) Open your books and start reading chapter thirteen. And pick up all that paper off the floor. Sit up straight, Earl"!

Mr. Johnson didn't realize it, but for a while he was blessed with the best class session held in his room since he began teaching ten years ago. He felt threatened, and he will undoubtedly go back to his old method of boring students on Monday. He only hopes the principal doesn't hear of the revolutionary ideas that his class came up with today. After all, they are only children. What do they know about life? He was surprised they hadn't brought up the subject of pollution. That's what these young anarchists are harping about lately.

Observed from the hallway through an open door into a classroom: A boy is sitting quietly with hands folded on his desk. A woman teacher stands over him, "You dummy, get out in the hall and stay there until I tell you to come back in here." He leaves the room. A few minutes later she goes out to him and sarcastically says, "You can come back to the class if you promise to control your emotions and calm down."

He answers softly, "I never said a word, Ma'm. You're doing all the yelling."

"Don't you dare talk back to me," she screams.

Woman teacher measuring seniors for caps and gowns: She calls out names and measurements (including chests) for both boys and girls. The girls are embarrassed. Teacher just laughs and continues to call loudly. One girl measures 37 inches and the boys whistle and applaud to show their appreciation.

Teacher's opening remark to class: "I don't want to be here anymore than you do. I know you don't like me, but I'm not overly fond of you, either."

Another teacher to class: "Don't tell me how to teach! What makes you think you're so smart? I don't see your name on my paychecks."

Another: "The next person who speaks without raising his hand for proper permission will be sent to the office."

Huge male teacher: "If that little bastard shows up in my room without his hair cut today, I'm going to kick him all the way down the stairs."

Teacher to superintendent: "Mr. Jones, I found a fairly new tape recorder in a closet, but it doesn't work. Could we get it repaired?"

Superintendent: "I didn't get it fixed, because it never gets used."

Teacher: "How can we use it if it doesn't work?" etc.

Student: "That Mrs. Sample must take mean pills. She exercises your stomach and bowels rather than your mind."

Small girl in tears to teacher: "You put your own shitty problems on the board. Please, oh please leave me alone!"

Teacher to girls whispering in the back of room: "All right, girls, obviously I seem to be boring you. Now you can tell the whole class what you were whispering about."

Student: "We were just wondering if the Puritans enjoyed sex."

Laughter from class.

Teacher: "All right, since you think it is so funny, we will all stay fifteen minutes after school and laugh."

Male teacher obviously blushing and uncomfortable: "Why don't you grow up and stop snickering at the mention of sex? You should be able to discuss it without becoming embarrassed."

Two female teachers: "I'll bet that little bitch is on the pill or else she would be knocked up higher than a kite by now. She doesn't fool me one bit. The first chance I get, I'm going to bomb her right out of there. If she passes my class, believe me, she will earn it the hard way."

Answer: "Good for you, Doris. I can tell by just looking at a girl whether or not she is decent! These girls can pull the old Oedipus trick on the men teachers, but I see right though them."

Another male teacher: "This is the last time they are going to stick me with remedial math. They can shove that general math. How come I get stuck with all the dumb kids? If a kid can't hack algebra, he will never make it in life."

My brother-in-law was deemed a sparrow while moving through the elementary and secondary school systems as a youth. He was a dutiful "stick man" in rhythm band. He dropped out of high school and joined the navy in WWII where he received his GED. After the war, he owned stereo/high fidelity stores in Champaign, Carbondale, and Peoria, Illinois. He comfortably retired at age 50. He never had a course in algebra.

Part Six

1967-1983

We returned to Springfield, South Dakota where I taught for 17 years at Southern State College, which became a branch of the University of South Dakota. The movies during this era were "The Graduate", "Patton", "The Godfather", "The Sting", and "One Flew Over the Cuckoo's Nest".

Robert Kennedy was killed by an Arab, Sirhan Sirhan. Alabama Governor George Wallace was shot be Arthur Bremer. Martin Luther King was assassinated in Memphis. The mother of Martin Luther King was shot to death as she played the organ in church.

Joe Namath and the New York Jets beat Baltimore in the 1969 Super Bowl.

Archie Bunker of "All In The Family" was America's most popular bigot.

President Nixon vetoed a $19 billion appropriation for health education and anti-poverty on the premise that such expenditure would aggravate inflation. This included milk money for school kids and the Head Start program.

The voting age was reduced to 18!!! Finally!!!

President Nixon had promised to end the Viet Nam War. Instead, he sent troops into Cambodia. This brought out hundreds of thousands of war protesters. Four students were killed at

Kent State University. Nixon called the student protesters "bums".

April 30, 1975, South Viet Nam surrendered to the communists, ending the Viet Nam War.

Vice President Spiro Agnew resigned and pleaded "nolo contendere" on charges of tax evasion on payments made to him by Maryland contractors. Agnew was sentenced to three years probation and fined $10,000.

President Nixon said he would pay $432,787 in back taxes after a joint Congressional committee found him liable.

Quis Custodiet Ispos Custodes? Who is guarding the guardians? Who is watching the watchers?

I was invited to give the commencement address in a small town in the West River country of South Dakota. This was cattle country. I was surprised to see how many families and friends showed up to help celebrate the graduation of these young people. The gym was packed. I was seated on the stage next to Father Flaherty. He was there to offer the traditional Invocation and Benediction. He leaned over to me and said, "Keep it short and they will love you."

I had just begun my speech, when a small boy, perhaps about four years old, came out of the audience and walked straight toward the stage. He was dressed in typical cowboy fashion: jeans, shirt, and boots. Naturally, no one is listening to anything I'm saying. All eyes are on this little boy. People are smiling and pointing. He makes it up the stairs on all fours. Then walks over and stands right beside me at the podium. Cute kid. His mother finally appears in front of the stage. I take him by the hand and lead him to her.

They disappear back into the crowd. Back to my speech. There is an old saying that states, "A sparrow fluttering inside a temple is an antagonist no theologian can cope with." My antagonist wasn't a sparrow. It was a bat. It dived from the rafters and swooped low just above the heads of the people, then back to the rafters. It made a second and lower dive. Boys tried to catch it in their hats. Women screamed. They knew that if a bat gets in your hair, the only way to get it out is to cut all your hair off. Everyone knows that.

Back to the speech. After order was somewhat established, I began to hear and feel a strange rumbling. Oh my God, not an earthquake here in South Dakota? It turned out to be a freight train. The engineer dutifully hit the horn at the street crossing. After about twelve minutes of utter chaos, I heeded Father Flaherty's advice. I closed by pleading, "There is one very important thing I would be pleased and proud to have you remember about this day. Your future will — — — — — — — — —." My lips were moving but no sound was coming from the microphone. Someone had tripped over the cord behind the stage and pulled the plug. Murphy's Law ruled. Anything that can go wrong will go wrong. A speaker's nightmare.

Afterwards, I was overwhelmed by firm handshakes of well-wishers complimenting me and thanking me for my wonderful speech. The president of the school board said, "I've lived here all my life, and that's the best speech I ever heard. The only thing that could top that would be an inch and a half of rain."

A woman approached me and asked, "Would you please join us at our house for lunch right away? It won't be a big deal, but you have to eat something before you drive home." I figured it would be bad manners, even rude, not to accept. When I arrived at the designated house, they could have used a cop to direct traffic. Her 'little lunch' turned out to be a potluck. I never saw so much food along with an outdoor barbecue topped off with homemade ice cream.

I have loved being invited to be the main speaker at organization and club dinners, athletic banquets, patriotic events, and commencements. I was keynote speaker for "Current Trends", an annual workshop for South Dakota elementary and secondary teachers who want to keep up on the latest trends in education. They invited me to come back the next year to give the closing address. In 1978, I was asked to be the banquet speaker for Loyalty Day at the Veterans of Foreign Wars Post 628 in Sioux Falls. It is the second-largest V.F.W. Post in America. I was invited to return as banquet speaker four years later in 1982. I'm the only person to do this twice. I was awarded the honor of being the speaker for the U.S. Marine Corps' 200th anniversary dinner and ball in Omaha. Ex-marines and marines were invited from a four-state area.

Sounds like an ego trip, but I want to point out that I'll always love, cherish, and remember my early speaking experience in that tiny West River town many moons ago. It was special.

In 1967 the president of Southern State College called and offered me a position on his faculty. I hadn't applied there, and his phone call caught me by surprise. I would be teaching in the education and psychology department. I considered this an honor and an unexpected opportunity to teach at the college level. Especially at my alma mater. I accepted.

We moved to Springfield. Back in Jack Rich's neat little hometown. I was never so happy and eager to begin a school year. We bought a big two-story house...one of the oldest in town. Dr Keeling had built it in 1891. A solid, lovely home. We paid $11,300 for it. Made a down payment of $1,300 and borrowed $10,000 from the bank with a promise to make payments for twenty years. Our kids were starting high school where I had taught in the early 1950's. We were so happy. We settled in.

During the pre-school workshop in late August, the president called me to his office. He informed me that the person hired as director of student life would be a couple of weeks late in reporting. This person would be coming from the East Coast. "Dr. Simmons has had some minor surgery. He will be here as soon as possible. With your experience as a counselor, I would like you to fill in and be the acting director of student life for two weeks. Of course we can't pay you anything extra for this, so it will be in addition to your regular teaching assignment."

Impulsively, I volunteered, "I'll be more than happy to help out. No problem. If you need anything else, just let me know."

The two weeks turned out to be two months. In my opinion, this job is the worst and most time-consuming duty on a college campus. Problems in the dorms, any discipline, name it. I even had complaints from the local bar owner about students that wrote bad checks. I went to the president and let him know that what the students did off campus was not our business. Let the police handle these matters. He did agree with me. This 'temporary' duty soon found me serving on at least five different committees, which met either after school or after dinner. I rarely saw my family. Remember, I'm also teaching my assigned class load for which I am getting paid.

We are into October. Our Founders' Day Homecoming is coming up. Parade, football game with Yankton College, pheasant season opening, wonderful time of year. The phone rings. The president wants to see me right away.

I enter his office. I am facing the person that has the power of life or death. Remember the classic scenes from Peter Seller's Pink Panther when he drove his supervisor nuts? Dr. Millar was a good president, but he was prone to overreact on occasion. The first thing I noticed was that he was smoking and held a burning cigarette in each hand. Not a good sign.

"The president of Yankton College just called me. He said someone on this campus called their student body president and boasted that their mascot, a greyhound statue, was now on our campus. Their students are outraged and want their greyhound back. You have 24 hours to find and return it."

"Yes, Sir."

My cloak and dagger investigation produced nothing. I appealed to the students in my classes. I explained the situation, and they were delighted to hear of the dognapping. I also whined, "Fun is fun, but my job is on the line. I have a wife and two kids." No response. Dead end.

Then later that day, Pat McGill, one of our cheerleaders, came to my office. She spoke softly. "Some guys brought the greyhound for me to keep in my room. They said no one would ever think to look in my closet. It's not very big. Bring something to wrap it in. Come over to the dorm and get it. I can't tell you who the guys are. I won't be very popular anyway."

"You have my word. You can tell them I did some detective work that led to you, and I threatened you. Thanks, Pat. You did the right thing."

She sighed. "There's just one more little thing."

"Yes?"

"They probably won't be too thrilled when they see the greyhound is painted our school colors, red and white."

I sped post haste to Yankton College. Their president was not amused. He shook his head and folded his hands on his desk. "You know I could press charges."

I apologized profusely. "You really don't want to do that. It would only exacerbate things. Why not turn this dog over to your art department? I'll bet someone could repaint it to make it look better than ever."

"Okay, but I want you to know that this is the kind of behavior I could expect from that bunch of rowdy people you have on your campus. Our students would never do such things. Say hello to Dr. Millar for me."

I bit my tongue. After all, I had come as a mediator, hat in hand. Mission accomplished.

I still wasn't off the hook. I reported back to Dr. Millar. I related the highlights...I didn't really lie, but omitted many details and got right to the crux of the matter. I quoted Yankton College's president by saying, "You know, he said our students were a bunch of rowdies and ruffians." I knew this would strike a nerve. So I paraphrased a bit.

"He said that?" Dr. Millar only had one cigarette burning at this time. "Good work, I'm proud of you." He didn't ask for names. Didn't ask how I solved the problem.

The next morning, I'm up bright and early. It's a beautiful sunrise. I'm so relieved to have the greyhound crisis behind me. I decide to walk to work. It is 7:30 a.m. and I'm confronted in front of the gym by my old idol and football coach, Jack Martin. He is a South Dakota legend. He spent his life as a football coach and athletic director at our school. He had been an army captain who saw combat in the Philippines in WWII. He was known for his locker room tongue-lashings. I always felt that I escaped his wrath because of my war record in the marines, plus I was the oldest guy on the team.

Forget favoritism. "I've been waiting for you."

I respected and loved this man dearly. He stood in front of me with arms folded across his chest. Football was his life. He was a Catholic, a husband, a father of five children. He could see the football field from his office window. I think he resented a squirrel or a rabbit on his field. The field would later be named Jack Martin Field in his honor. The field was 120 yards of lush green grass. Of course, this was before artificial turf and indoor domes.

"Something wrong, Coach?"

"Come with me."

He led me across the street, through the south entrance to the football field, across the track, under the goal post, and onto the field. We marched briskly and silently to the 50-yard line. "Look at this! Look what they did."

It was ugly. Someone had sneaked onto the field last night, poured gasoline in the outline of a big "YC", and torched it.

I had never seen Coach Martin so distraught. His shoulders slumped. I felt as though I was viewing a body at a funeral. He finally spoke. "This was no doubt some of those worthless football players that they recruit from the East Coast. What a bunch of riffraff they have on that campus. Our students would never do such a thing. What are we going to do about this? We have a game here tomorrow."

Here we go again. God, I loved this job as 'acting' Director of Student Life.

"Coach, no way can you repair this by game time. Why not leave it just as it is. Just think how you can use this to fire your team up? (No pun intended.) And wait until our students, alumni, and fans see this. That's not all; I wouldn't dignify what they did by protesting to their coach or president. That would be a class act on your part. The grass will grow back. This too shall pass."

I lucked out again. We won the game.

It is ironic that neither school exists today. Yankton College is now a Federal Prison. Our school in Springfield was converted to a South Dakota State Prison, complete with razor wire.

I always told my students that when I lectured, I tried to present facts. When I offered an opinion I called them Barhamisms. Barhamism: Today if you see a new building going up, there is a good chance it will be a prison, a bank, or a pizza parlor. Fact: since 1980, the percentage of arrests of boys and young men has stabilized or even decreased for violent crimes. At the same time, the percentage of arrests of girls and young women has increased 74%. Check the police reports in the newspapers and you will find about half of the people arrested for writing bad checks, D.U.I.'s, disorderly conduct, speeding, and assault are females. When I go to our cabin in Wisconsin, the Interstate speed limits are 75 in South Dakota, 70 in Minnesota, and 65 in Wisconsin. I set my cruise control accordingly. When I see a small red car that is rapidly coming from behind, I assume it will be a young female driver. They blow past me, and I'm correct most of the time.

Since my math and science teachers neglected to use meaningful examples of how this stuff could be used, I based my teaching philosophy on examples. When learning terms I constantly asked, "What does that really mean? How can we use this? Who can give me a personal example of this?"

Students enjoyed being involved. It made things fun and interesting. I was the catalyst, but I never knew how each class would react. Okay, I write "avarice" on the board. "Who can define this?"

"Greed".

"Good. Make it personal?"

Mark says, "My grandpa died a few weeks ago. My mom and her brother inherited everything grandpa had. They decided to sell his house and split the money. One night my uncle came to grandpa's house with his truck, dug up all the shrubs in the yard and took them home and landscaped his yard. It left big holes all over grandpa's yard. My mom was furious. They met at grandpa's house and got into a big fight. They were shouting at each other in the kitchen. I was in the bedroom and was looking in some drawers to see if I might find some cigarettes. Here were four one hundred dollar bills. Mom and my uncle were being greedy, so I just stuck the money in my pocket. Grandpa would have wanted me to do it. I'll bet he was smiling."

"Anyone see one of the three defense mechanisms at work here? Mary?"

"You bet. Rationalization, sour grapes. Mark is making excuses for his behavior."

"Well taken. Keep in mind that Mark is not on trial here. I wonder how many of you good people might have done the same thing. This probably won't change Mark's mind because of a factor we call cognitive dissonance. Anyone?"

No volunteers. I write the term on the board. "This is the tendency for individuals to reject or ignore evidence that is in conflict with conclusions they have already reached. Example?"

"People who vote a straight party ticket, even they know their candidate is a rotten, two-faced politician.

"Anyone else?"

"Could you stretch it far enough to include close-minded people that think their religion or race is superior to all others?"

"Perhaps, but now you bring up another interesting term." I write 'ethnocentrism' on the board. "This is primarily a belief in your racial superiority. The Hitler thing sums that up very well."

Someone offers, "Do you think that sometimes people have already made up their minds that a person is guilty or not guilty even before they serve on a jury?"

"Unfortunately that's very possible." I'm always looking for hands in the air. I hate teachers that ignore questions. "Yes, Mark?"

"I was thinking you might be an example of what we have been talking about."

Kung Fu was a popular TV program during this era. I responded, "Careful, now. These have not been complimentary terms. Where does it say, Grasshopper, you make fool of teacher?"

"It's obvious you don't like the Japanese. After all these years, you're not likely to change your mind."

"That's a valid, astute observation. My marine friends of WWII feel the same way. The Nips weren't nice, so we had to kill 'em. Hundreds of 'em. I will never forgive them. There is an old saying in the marines. 'To err is human. To forgive is divine. Neither is U.S. Marine Corps policy.'"

"Let's talk about euphemisms. Define it. Put it in your own words."

"That's when you substitute a nice word for one that sounds offensive. Instead of saying my mom died, and she has been dead for three years, you say, 'I lost my mom. She passed away three years ago.'"

"In the funeral business, they refer to the room where the body is viewed as the slumber room."

I added, "Probably in death, people are most careful to be reverent and not offend anyone."

"How about when you put your dog 'to sleep'?"

"Obese or a bit heavy rather than fat?"

"We could cite many examples, couldn't we?"

"How about body secretions? Guys sweat and women perspire."

I suggested that when you get into bodily functions it comes down to what are accepted and good manners. Nothing spoils a nice dinner in a romantic setting more than a loud, obnoxious, foul mouth.

"Question?"

"Who really determines what is in good taste?"

I turn the question back to the class. Let's take the word 'urinate'. Don't be shy. You all have heard substitute words especially those made up by mothers for their little kids. Like what?"

"Tinkle".

"Witter".

"Swish".

You all know and have heard or have read on public bathroom walls descriptive words that are vulgar.

I asked, "Remember in the movie "Gone With The Wind" years ago when Clark Gable uttered that famous line, 'Frankly, my dear, I don't give a damn.'?" It shocked the nation. A well-known national figure was in trouble recently. I read where someone was quoted in the newspaper as saying he was up to his neck in feces. That's pushing the fine line. As you all know, I love quotes that have substance and make people think. I'm interested primarily in what was said. If I said I don't give a rat's derriere who said it, I would be speaking euphemistically."

Shifting gears, "What is pedophilia?"

"Getting your sexual kicks from molesting children."

"What would you do with these people? Cathy?"

Use a knife and do that thingy on their brain."

"You mean a lobotomy."

"Whatever."

"Yes, Jim?"

"Stick 'em in the toughest prison. The inmates will take care of them. They all hate those guys."

I look at my watch. Time to dismiss. I end every lecture with, "Thank you for coming to class today."

It is 1976.

On a clear autumn afternoon in 1927, President Calvin Coolidge left the comfort of his automobile and rode horseback the remaining three miles to the base of a mountain called Rushmore.

There, with his characteristic dignity, Coolidge stated, "We have come here to dedicate a cornerstone that was laid by the Almighty. It is but natural that such a work begin with George Washington, for with him begins that which is truly characteristic of America."

President Coolidge then handed Gutzon Borglum, the sculptor, a set of drills, and the carving of the world's most colossal sculpture began. The task ended 14 years later.

This Shrine of Democracy will attract more than three million visitors in the nation's bicentennial year of 1976. But I will be hosting the most exclusive party of the summer (August 6th to 8th) in the shadow of Mount Rushmore. Thirty-five U.S. marines will answer roll call at the State Game Lodge, the summer White House for President Coolidge and President Eisenhower.

Working from a roster of names heavily edited by battle and time, the guest list will include 50 per cent of the living members of K Company, 9th Marines, 3rd Marine Division of World War II. Of the 275 men originally assigned K Company, only 70 left World War II alive. While serving as part of the famous Striking 9th Marines, K Company suffered 100 percent casualties, and nearly every survivor holds at least one Purple Heart.

Thirty years later most people have forgotten about the battles of Bougainville, Guam and Iwo Jima. But not the 35 marines who will be meeting in the Black Hills of South Dakota for their seventh annual reunion. Eight survivors met six years ago in St. Louis, and the number has steadily grown with meetings in Memphis, Dallas, Houston, Tulsa and New Orleans.

We don't meet to glorify war. Many have saved each other's lives, but there are no heroes. This is a special group steeped in camaraderie. We meet to re-experience the bond we shared during those times of extreme emotion-fear, joy, hope, and grief. There isn't an atheist among us, and we ponder why we were chosen to live when so many died. We feel that every day we have lived since the war has been a dividend, and we thank God for this.

Our country today suffers from a climate of pessimism and public distrust of government. Much of this was brought on by a very unpopular war in Vietnam in which we changed our purposes several times, indicating that as a nation we did not know why we fought there.

    The men of K Company are outdated outcasts from an old war. We never questioned the motives of our war. The sneak attack on Pearl Harbor gave us a cause to fight for. But not without paying a terrible price. We feel that our country buried quality men on battlefields of foreign lands in World War II.

    We were trained to kill. We did it well. For 30 years the memories have been locked in the dark closets of our minds, burned into our skulls. So we meet, talk, listen and share, because we care about each other. An aura of genuineness is created that could be compared with the tiny silken blue and yellow threads that run through our paper money. Invisible, but that extra something that sets it apart from counterfeit imitations.

    It's not easy to forget bodies that lay rotting in the sun. The echo that trails behind the staccato voice of a machine gun. The screams of men. A young marine holding his dead buddy in his arms, rocking back and forth crying, "Why, why?" Finding a friend in a foxhole with his eyes open, a cigarette burning between his fingers, a small blue hole in his forehead and the back of his head gone.

    K Company had its baptism of fire on Bougainville in the Solomon Islands. We again feel the flames as words and stories emerge. Somebody reminds us of Cape Torokina where we landed, Nov. 1st, 1943, Hill 1000, the Numa-Numa Trail, the 58 days of jungle, swamp, mud, mosquitoes, and malaria. Colonel Hyde, a Texan, recalls the patrol when Lt. Freeman was wounded and received a broken jaw. Gentry says, "I was covering the rear of that patrol with my B.A.R." (Gentry re-enlisted and froze his feet in the Korean War.) Hyde says, "I suppose we were a little rough on Freeman that day, but he wanted us to leave him out there on the trail. He would have bled to death, or the Nips would have killed him for sure."

    It's difficult to believe that 30 years later I would be visiting with a handful of survivors from that patrol. I never dreamed that K Company's Lt. Orville Freeman would become governor of Minnesota and secretary of agriculture. But Jim Stussie, now a Circuit Court judge in St. Louis, said that Lt. Freeman had told him in New Zealand, "After the war, I'm going to graduate from law school and become governor of Minnesota."

Bobby Givines, Oklahoma, was only 14 when he lied about his age and joined the Marine Corps. After the Bougainville campaign, we went to Guadalcanal to rest and lick our wounds. Givines' true age was discovered, but it was too late to send him home. Bobby grew up faster than most kids.

When we talk of Guam we recall July 21st, 1944. We were a veteran outfit making the first wave assault. We remember the red dust, the mountains, the capital city of Agana in rubble, and the pride of seeing the Stars and Stripes flying over the Piti Navy Yard for the first time since December 1941. Lawhon remembers being severely wounded. He should. He spent three years in the hospital getting repaired. I lost the vision in one eye on Guam. At the same time I lost the best friend I ever had. Jack Rich's memorial flag flies over the football stadium at the University of South Dakota at Springfield every homecoming afternoon.

Melton remembers Guam. His platoon was caught in an ambush, and Lee, Hardin, and McCracken were killed. Melton was shot through the neck and chest. He was bleeding badly and thought he was dying. He tells us about it now: "I wondered what John Wayne would do right then. I decided to have a last cigarette. Do you think I could find a match? I could hear some Nips coming, so I took a grenade and pulled the pin. I was going to take some of them with me." A corpsman found him unconscious, slumped against the live active grenade with the handle still on.

The war rolled on and the attrition and the death.

K Company sailed from Guam to Iwo Jima on the USS Leedstown. Mount Suribachi loomed ominously on the horizon. The island's shape could be compared with a pear, a pork chop, or a dripping ice cream cone. It was a desert of rock—a barren, ugly, but important island. It was also the bloodiest, fiercest fight in the history of the Marine Corps: February 1945—every officer in the 3rd Battalion killed or wounded—faces stained black and yellow by the volcanic ash and sulphur of the island. George Wayman, Missouri, remembers lying in a shell hole for 28 hours as his blood seeped in to the sand. Troy Young, a Navy medical corpsman, found him, applied a sulfa dressing, gave him a half-grain of morphine, a pint of albumen. 'Doc' is the only non-marine who attends our reunions.

Clyde McGinnis, our exec officer, was a former track star at Oklahoma who had to run against Glen Cunningham. Now a sporting goods dealer, he hosted our 1974 reunion in Tulsa. He stood at the banquet table and said, "This is the proudest moment of my life." His voice broke, and tears rolled down his cheeks. After a pause he continued, "I'm sorry, I didn't want to do that." Then Jim Boman, a retired rural mail carrier from Missouri, offered a prayer. That gruff old silver-thatched platoon sergeant softly stated that we could feel the presence of all K Company men with us in spirit at that moment. When he said, "Amen," 25 whispered amens hung in the air.

We come from all over the United States, but there is a distinct Texas flavor in K Company. Harwell and Stengel, who were foxhole buddies, live in Houston. Harwell claims he dug every foxhole they shared during those three years. Stengel vehemently denies this. We all agree with Harwell.

War wounds heal, but scars remain. No one complains of the probing fingers of nagging pain, subtle reminders after all these years. We laugh a lot. We agree that President Truman's decision to use The Bomb saved countless lives on both sides. At that time the terrible fighting still raged half past dark, and more. We were less than thrilled by Emperor Hirohito's recent visit to the United States and his homage at the Tomb of the Unknown Soldier. We realize this is an Archie Bunker attitude, but some things we can't forget.

Willie Schustz organized our New Orleans reunion. He raced around tending our needs like a mother hen. No easy task for a man with one leg. He caught his breath and said, "It's a good life. It's a good country." David Thompson and his charming wife flew in from their home in Hawaii. Charm and love strike without wounds, win wars without casualties. David's wife, Mitsue, is Japanese/American.

One by one they will drift into the game lodge. Pradt and Hickman, also from Texas, Sigman, the Oldsmobile man from Memphis. Rondo, the Mississippi gentleman who paints tall towers that other men shy away from. Neaveill, excited about coming from Illinois for his first reunion. Martin, the Iowa farmer who will pilot his own plane. And Fullerton, who comes from Florida. His eye surgery wasn't as successful as mine. Gentry, the Houston drug squad detective, who had a femoral artery removed as a result of his frozen feet in Korea, underwent surgery and had 250 stitches taken. He'll probably miss the reunion. Faces from the past.

I'm excited about bringing the men of K Company to the Black Hills of South Dakota. I can hardly wait to lead that crew of gimpy old men to the foot of Mount Rushmore. Pictures on postcards can't evoke the emotions they will experience when those four great somber faces seem to reach down to them. If it should be raining, tears will fall from the huge, incredibly sensitive eyes. I know these old marines. They won't be able to leave without looking back for a parting glimpse.

We are incurable optimists. There must be some way of restoring confidence, of rekindling a spark of belief in this nation's essential goodness. Our hearts ache. Perhaps a messiah?

Lt. Pat Caruso, New Jersey, was one of our platoon leaders. He was evacuated from Iwo to Hawaii and placed in a hospital barrack next to another that housed captured wounded Japanese. Caruso wrote in a diary 30 years ago, "I had to pass their barracks on the way to the mess hall. It didn't take long before I began to recognize some of their faces as they peered through their windows. Our eyes would meet through that barbed wire, and a faint smile or a reluctant gesture of acceptance developed between us. Though there was no exchange of words, I felt each of us began to realize that the other was human."

There is hope.

Another class. I write 'ecumenical' on the board. "This can be summed up in a single word. Worldwide. Ecumenism would strive to unite religions through cooperation and understanding. Good luck. How about a personal example? Grace?"

"I post notices around campus that there will be a meeting in Main Hall tonight at 7:00 p.m. List the reason or cause. It will involve an ecumenical prayer service and everyone is welcome."

"Excellent. Now I have to tell you a story. When I was 37 years old, I was hired as football coach at Buena Vista College in Iowa. It was a private Presbyterian school. The basketball coach was Presbyterian, the athletic director was Presbyterian, I was

Presbyterian. The A.D. was one of the finest educators I ever knew. One of his duties was to make travel arrangements, hotels, meals in advance. Our opening game involved a road trip. A couple of days before the trip, he asked me to find out how many fish dinners he should order for Friday's meal. "Just get a show of hands at practice today."

I'm new on campus. I can go along with a joke. He is setting me up. I know that there won't be any fish dinners for a Presbyterian football team. Everyone that goes to a school named Wesleyan anywhere in the country is a Methodist. All students enrolled at Notre Dame are Catholic. Everyone knows that. So I humor him. I gather my squad around me and with a straight face I ask, "How many fish dinners for Friday?" About a dozen hands go up. I could see that they are serious.

I ask, "Why are all you Catholics playing football for Buena Vista?"

"We got a better deal here."

"It's close to home."

"I like it here. It's a good school."

Pretending that I hadn't discovered something for the first time in my life, I was serious when I said, "Good answers. We are a team. We are family."

Father McCoy was probably our number one fan. He rarely missed a practice and never missed a home game. It was mid-October and we had our Homecoming game coming up with Wartburg. They were the defending Iowa Conference champions. They also were a veteran team riding a 15-game winning streak and featured a Little All-American quarterback. This awesome Lutheran school was set to roll into town Saturday.

We had injuries to key players. Our best running back, our fullback, and our excellent defensive back were on the sidelines. Not even in uniform. At the alumni dinner the evening before the game, I listed the injuries and extolled the credentials of this powerful team that we would face tomorrow.

Saturday morning pre-game, I walk into our locker room and find Red Burnet passing out cigars. He had been up all night while his wife had their first baby. He will be my starting fullback and hasn't had a wink of sleep. An omen?

God smiled on us the first half. Wartburg shot itself in the foot mercifully. They dominated the game as expected. Every drive resulted in a fumble or a pass interception.

We seldom had the ball. They rolled up unreal yardage without scoring. We were lucky to make a first down. On the last play of the first half, they kicked a 40-yard field goal, and the half ended, 3-0.

As I walked off the field toward the locker room, Father McCoy appeared magically at my side. He asked, "Would you like me to go to the church and ask the nuns to offer a prayer for you?"

We never broke stride. I said, "Forget it. I don't have the time now."

"But you can't believe what they can do when they put their minds to it."

"Forget it, Father."

The second half starts. We receive. I decide to gamble. The first football player I met when I took over the team in June...was a halfback in the hospital with a broken ankle. He was the victim of a motorcycle accident. He hadn't played a minute of the season as he recuperated. It really wasn't a smart move. He stood beside me, as I put my arm around his shoulder. "Get ready. This will be the first play you will be involved in this season. Are you ready?" (Pressure.)

"Yes, Coach."

We call screen pass left. This means we let the defense stream in while our linemen drift off the left sideline and block downfield. Our guys execute perfectly. Our broken leg halfback, on the first time he touches the ball, goes 60 yards to the 2-yard line. From there, we score and it's 7-3.

They fumble the kick off. We recover on the 30. Our bleary-eyed fullback seems obsessed. Can a new baby do this? Adrenalin? We put together a good series. We score. It's 14-3 and the second half is barely underway. Wartburg isn't used to being behind in a game. Everything goes wrong for them. In the fourth quarter, they are backed up by our fired up defense. They attempt a pass and our big tackle bats it. It comes down in his arms and he rumbles in for a touchdown. We win the game 20-3. A routine miracle?

As I made my way through the celebrating crowd on the field, Father McCoy caught up with me. He told me that he had said a prayer for me at halftime.

I asked, "I don't suppose you would tell me what you said?"

"Why not? Dear Lord, would you please help these lowly Presbyterians just this once? Don't let them be humiliated by these Lutherans."

"I loved this man, but I never really knew for sure when he was serious. If so, we had a priest praying for the Presbyterians to beat the Lutherans. You can't get any more ecumenical than that. Thank you for coming to class today."

Our students who were to become teachers took Educational Psychology for eight weeks and then did their student teaching the last eight weeks of the semester. I assigned them to various elementary and secondary schools. I also supervised some of them as they did their student teaching.

It was my intent to relate personal examples of experiences of former cadet teachers. One student teacher shared this incident, which I in turn, shared with my class. A first grade boy brought his cousin to school as a visitor. The little boy approached his teacher and said, "My cousin has to go to the bathroom."

"All right. But you go with him, because you know where it is."

They were gone a bit longer than she had expected. She was about to check on them when they returned. When she had a private opportunity, she inquired, "What took you so long?"

"He couldn't find it."

"That's why I sent you with him. You were to show him where the bathroom is."

"No I mean he couldn't find it. He put his shorts on backwards this morning."

Another example. A teacher was informed that a father of one of her second graders had a heart attack and was still in the hospital. The little boy was having a bad day in school. The teacher consoled him with, "I know you must be worried about your dad in the hospital."

"Yes. And my shoelace broke, but that's okay. I still have the other piece."

More classroom talk. Barhamism: The woman I most admire in American history has to be Eleanor Roosevelt. Partly because she visited Guadalcanal of all places when I was there in WWII. That makes me biased. I have no idea how she got there. It was early in the war and she put her life on the line to look up and visit her son, Jimmy, who led a highly respected marine raider battalion. This woman was way ahead of her time. She was an outspoken writer, diplomat, and humanitarian. I'm pretty sure that she said, "No one can make me feel inferior without my consent." And she might have said, "Everyone is ignorant, only on different subjects."

When I was the football coach at Rhinelander High School in Wisconsin in the late 1950's, I had a student in my American history class by the name of Jerry Harper. These were the Happy Days that later became a big hit on TV. Our school was full of Ron Howards. Jerry was the perfect stereotype. Black leather jacket, ducktail hairstyle, shirt collar rolled up. Actually these were great years, but as usual, high school kids were thought of as threats. Jerry was not a problem in school. He simply typified a group that wasn't interested in the things he was supposed to learn. So he rode along on straight D's. Just enough to pass each subject. When I asked him a question in class, he would shrug and answer, "I don't know," even before I finished the question. It was frustrating.

Since I was the football coach, I was awarded the dubious honor of supervising the biggest study hall in the school. The room actually was the auditorium, with a stage at one end. Naturally, the back of the room was higher so that the wooden floor slanted downward toward the stage. Desks were arranged so that there were several aisles between them. Students could drive a teacher crazy by rolling a marble or a steel ball bearing down the aisle to the stage. They also could start a coughing spree. Sporadic at first, but leading to a crescendo. Today, a study hall of this size would have several teachers in charge. I never had to deal with these problems, but other teachers did. After taking roll, I liked to stand at the back of the room where I could survey the big picture. Students that turned and looked at me frequently were usually guilty of something. I also admired the view from the many windows. The woods pressed against the building on the east side. The fall colors were gorgeous. In the winter, the huge snowflakes wafted down to nestle on the pine boughs. I compared this scene with a South Dakota blizzard where the wind howls unmercifully. I thought a teacher in this study hall had as much chance of catching the culprit that rolls a marble down the aisle as a person trying to catch a snowflake in a South Dakota blizzard. My salary was awful, but the kids of the Fabulous fifties were wonderful. Once in a great while a young boy would get a bit noisy or create a mild disturbance. This was my turf. I made it a point to never call out a name, never shout. My strategy paid off. I walked the aisles quietly, slowly and perhaps several minutes after this unruly lad had been a pain, I would stop beside him and put my arm around his shoulder. Good old Coach. Nice friendly gesture. I smiled and whispered in his ear, "I want you to smile while I'm talking to you." There is a cordlike muscle that extends from the neck to the shoulder. Still smiling, I grasped this cord between my thumb and fingers I squeezed until I knew it hurt but not enough for him to cry out. This got his attention. Then I took a page from Sgt. Daly's marine boot camp book. I repeated, "Keep smiling. If you give me any more problems, I'll have to take you out behind the school in these beautiful woods and hurt you." I had few problems. Of course, I wouldn't dare touch the girls, but in those days girls were not a problem. Today, at least 50% of the discipline problems are girls.

Jerry Harper was in my study hall. Never a problem. Always busy reading, but I noticed it was never a school textbook. I checked with his friends. "What is Jerry reading all the time?"

"Are you serious? He's reading everything he can get his hands on about the Civil War"

The next day as I patrolled the study hall, I stopped by Jerry's desk. I spoke very softly. "I hear you are a Civil War buff."

"Who told you that?"

"Hey, I know everything," I lied.

"So?"

"We are about ready to get into the Civil War in history class. How would you like to take over the class for a day? Do anything you like. At least lead the discussion?"

I fully expected him to say, "I'll tell you what you can do with your history class." And where to put it.

He pleasantly surprised me. "I'd like that."

"How long will it take you to get ready?"

"How about tomorrow?"

I was a bit apprehensive about this new venture, but after all, if things didn't go well, I could bail him out and take over.

The next day, after history class roll taking, I announced, "Today we are going to start a unit on the Civil War." Groans. "We also will have a guest lecturer. Jerry?" For a few seconds, absolute silence. All eyes turn to Harper He gets up and walks to the front of the class. Quickly, applause, whistles, and a "Way to go Jer" erupt. I walk to the back of the room and sit down. I think, "What have I done? I hope he isn't embarrassed."

This sixteen-year-old boy picked up a piece of chalk from the tray, proceeded to list dates and events, and deliver one of the best lectures I have ever witnessed. No notes. His description was so graphic; it mesmerized a room full of teenagers. Not an easy task. Avoiding dates that would be forgotten, he described battles that began at dawn with dense fog in swampy areas. The temperature, the filthy, ragged uniforms, the age of the bugler and where he was from, the officer's background, the name and color of his horse.

Questions from the class. Hands waving in the air. Normally, the students wanted to know exactly when the class period was about to end. Notebooks would slam shut, and they were poised to flee into the hallways for four minutes of freedom between classes. Not today. The time flew so fast; the bell took them by surprise. I caught Jerry. "Do you have enough material for tomorrow?"

"I think I can manage another day."

"Okay, you're on again."

The next morning, I checked my mailbox in the principal's office. There were two secretaries in the outer office. They handled a zillion duties. The superintendent, principal, teachers, could be absent with no problem. But let just one of the two secretaries be absent, it was chaos. And if both were gone, I swear the school would close for the day. One of these miracle workers spied me. "Coach, Mr. Evans would like to see you in his office."

I entered the sanctuary. Richard Evans was a typical harried principal. An excellent administrator. A friend. "Close the door." Not a good sign. "Have a chair." Another bad sign. He is always busy, and he knows I have a first hour class. "I hear that Harper is teaching your history class."

How does he know this? Over a thousand teenagers in this high school, and he knows what one kid did yesterday.

I'm already on defense. "I wouldn't say he is teaching my class. He did share some information on the Civil War with my class yesterday. It's sort of a hobby with him."

"Is he going to share some of his thoughts in your class again today?"

"Sort of."

"Need I remind you that we are not paying Harper to teach your class? We are paying you for this."

"I know, but..."

He interrupted. "I may drop in on your class this afternoon. "I'll only stay a few minutes. That's all."

One of the rules not included in the teachers' handbook was, "Thou shalt not let anyone other than thyself take roll each period." This was to guarantee that a student couldn't leave a friend off the absent list that was posted outside the door, so that he might skip that period. I ignored this mandate and naturally assigned a girl to take roll in each class. She had the seating chart, and I never considered asking a boy to do this. I rationalized this disobedience each time by knowing I was a 'traveling teacher'. This meant each time the bell rang, I had four minutes to pick up whatever stuff I could carry and race to another room for my next class. Some teachers had the luxury of staying in the same room all day.

Cecil was sort of a wimpy little guy that hung out with questionable friends. Let's just say his hair was a bit longer than the clean-cut youth you could trust. He surprised me with, "Mr. Barham, you only let girls take roll for you. Why can't I do that for you?"

"You really want to do this?" What is this kid's motive? I can monitor him closely. "Okay, get the seating chart from Betty. You start tomorrow." Cecil became my most trusted roll taker. Never made a mistake and enforced the tardy rule. They knew when they came into Cecil's room, they had better be in their seats, or they were sent to the office for a tardy slip.

Fifth period. American history. The first person to enter the room was Mr. Evans. "Where do you want me to sit?"

"There are four empty desks at the back of the room. We will sit there."

"Oh? I thought you would be up in front, teaching as usual." He emphasized the word 'teaching' and I thought he spoke wryly.

Only seconds before the tardy bell. Twenty-eight teenagers fly into the room just in time to spot Mr. Evans and quiet down. For some unknown reason he lifts the top of the desk he is sitting at and discovers it is nearly half full of sunflower seed hulls. It looks like a squirrel had hibernated or lived there for a lifetime. He took a small notepad from his pocket and scribbled something. He can't pin this on me, because other teachers use this room.

Cecil is busy standing at the front of the room, taking roll. More vigorous scribbling in the notepad. Not a good sign.

Jerry begins before Cecil is through roll taking. Chalk in hand; he soon fills the board with exciting events. He has one small eraser and it takes forever to erase several boards. I've never seen this at any other time, but a boy in the front row jumps up, grabs another eraser and cleans off the boards to save time. Just like yesterday, an enthralled captivated audience. It wasn't simply words. You could almost taste, smell, and feel the atmosphere. Again, hands were waving in the air. Mr. Evans was caught asking too many sincere questions. Jerry reprimanded him. "Mr. Evans, you have to wait your turn." The kids turned to look at their principal for being chastised. His reaction could set the tone for the rest of the class. He laughed, threw up both hands, and admitted, "I'm sorry, I just got carried away." Mr. Evans 'dropped in' for a few minutes and stayed the entire period for a week as Jerry shared his private world with his peers. The psychology of learning began to gnaw at me.

A few days later, I was in the gym. The school nurse was gone for some reason. A boy burst into my office and urged, "Come quick, a girl passed out in study hall." I suppose, because of my P.E. background, I was schooled in first aid, and was the logical person to take charge. In seconds, I was there. She was lying on the floor between the desks. Her face was ashen. Her skirt was nearly to her waist, and I later learned that another girl had pulled the skirt down somewhat out of modesty. She recovered as I arrived. I helped her into her seat just as a monitor from the hallway reached me. "Another girl just fainted in the home ec room. By the time I got there, the teacher had the girl in a chair with her head down between her legs. At this moment, the intercom crackled. This was the squawk box that interrupted classes with 'important' messages all day long. "Now hear this. This is your principal speaking. There will be no more fainting in the building today. I repeat: no more fainting." Another routine miracle.

It is a fact that people shout at each other even in close proximity if a loud sound is nearby. Like a chainsaw or a tractor. I was on the dock at our cabin, relaxed in a chair, soaking up sun. Two guys came by in a boat a hundred yards from me. One yelled at the other, "Get the harpoon; it's Moby Dick over there on the dock!" They could barely hear each other, but I heard easily as the sound carried over the water above the roar of their outboard motor.

I also heard interesting conversations in this manner from the showers in boys' locker rooms. Soon after the fainting episodes, one boy shouts to his friend as they are showering, "You know, when Cindy fainted in the study hall, everyone crowded around, so I stood on top of my desk so I could see what was going on. Wow! I never saw white panties with a yellow rose and three green leaves before."

"Ralph, you never saw any panties before."

Strange, but that conversation has remained with me for over fifty years. I didn't get a glimpse of what Ralph described, but I wonder if they still make white panties with yellow roses and green leaves?

Perhaps my most rewarding experience in nearly 35 years as an educator came in 1972. The University of South Dakota/Springfield broke a long-established custom by requesting a speaker for their commencement from the teaching faculty instead of inviting a dignitary from off campus. The graduating class departed from tradition when they chose me. I also broke tradition in my remarks to the graduates.

My theme was "Take The Time". I did not encourage them to invade the business and professional world for the usual benefits of a large paycheck to purchase material things. I suggested they take the time to enjoy life to the fullest, to enjoy the intangibles of life such as honesty, self-discipline, friendship, and love for one's fellow man.

I urged them to cultivate their friends and family. "Be good to your friends, because without them you would be a stranger. Too many times, I have seen friends and associates who have allowed their jobs to dominate their entire lives. I feel this is wrong. Children know too often what their elders have forgotten: that only people are irreplaceable. People and not possessions are the source of happiness. You must continue to re-evaluate priorities in life. Is money the only thing that motivates us? It's always sad to hear a friend complain of his lack of time to read a book or start a new hobby or do anything else he really enjoys. For if life offers no time for these simple pleasures, why are we working so hard? Ask today's child about the sun, and he will tell you it is 93 million miles from earth along with other scientific data. Yet, I feel it is our main purpose in education to teach him to appreciate the radiance of a sunset. A competitive society reveres those who succeed and fills its mental hospitals with those who fail. Our most prized possession is time. Queen Elizabeth's last words were, 'All my possessions for one more moment of time.' Our lives on earth compared to all time are only a fleeting moment. Take the time to write a letter, smell the flowers, or watch the birds. Remember this. Anytime you are so important you can't be replaced, the size of your funeral will probably be determined by the weather."

I concluded by saying, "Thank you for coming to your graduation today." This was met by laughter and applause. It was what they were waiting to hear. As an inside joke, it probably escaped the faculty and parents.

I'm sure there were parents that were not prepared for my comments. This four-year college diploma had cost big bucks. After the ceremony, the handshakes, the hugs, and the tears, a father approached me. "This is the second son I have put through college." The first impression I had was that he didn't say 'we'. Like they didn't have a mother? He continued, "My older son took a year off after college and joined the Peace Corps. He wasted a whole year of his life, when he could have started law school right away."

"Did he say he wasted a whole year of his life?"

"No. In fact, he claims it was one of the best things he ever did. I just don't understand young people today."

"Did he pursue law school?"

"Yeah, he's doing okay, but he wasted a whole year of his life." My message fell upon at least two deaf ears.

I also vaguely remember jabbing the parents with a thought. I frequently challenged my class with, "Wrap your little minds around this." I aimed at the parents with, "There has been an age-old debate as to which is more important, heredity or environment. I would like to offer a Barhamism. The frightening thing is that parents provide both."

My students enjoyed introspection. It seemed a though they hadn't taken the time to examine their own inward thoughts or feelings. I asked them to make two lists and head one 'I Like' and the other 'I Don't Like'. The options were never-ending. It gave them insight that perhaps they hadn't realized, and it helped me to better understand them.

I also asked them to write a poem. This usually drew moans and groans. They wouldn't admit it, but I think they felt obligated to protest. Some continued to bring me poems long after they had taken my class. I kept a few in my files.

An Indian girl wrote:

Thunder Storm
Why is Great Spirit angry?
Have I done him wrong?
I hear the thundering of his voice,
As he sheds his tears on Mother Earth.
Why is he crying? I s he distressed with the world?
No, He wants his creation to grow strong before his eyes.

The Wind
Where is my song?
Where is the wind?
Where has it gone?
Where has it been?

It howls across the prairie
Roars over the sea
Murmurs in a wheat field
Whispers through a tree.

It sings through a kite's tail
Sneaks past a cloud
Scatters leaves and hailstones
Paints illusions, still or loud.

Winter's wind will numb my toes
Spring's breeze plays hide and seek
Summer's air will warm my nose
While fall's may brush my cheek.

Yesterday I smelled the wind
Tomorrow it will touch me
Today, old friend, it can be heard
Unseen, unreal, unique.

Shade
Shade is a piece of the night
left clinging to trees and buildings
transformed into a quiet pool contrasting the day
and its confusion.
Shade fears the sun
and hides from it
welcoming creatures of the day
who seek refreshment or
solitude.

A young woman asked me, out of the blue, in the middle of a class, "We wanted to know what woman of the past century you most admired, and you didn't hesitate when you named Eleanor Roosevelt. Did you have other reasons besides the ones you told us?"

I responded with, "Let me tell you a story. One of my favorite cousins, Thurm Barham, served as an army sergeant in the Solomon Islands during World War II. He was chosen to be sent back to the United States to attend Officers' Candidate School. While Thurm was stationed on the East Coast, President Roosevelt died."

On the afternoon of April 12th, 1945, the President was in his 'second home', a cottage at the Georgia Warm Springs foundation. He was working in his study. Suddenly he said, "I have a terrific headache." In a few minutes he lost consciousness. His Negro valet and Philippino valet mess boy carried him to the bedroom. The 32nd President of the United States died of a massive cerebral hemorrhage."

For twelve years, in war and peace, Roosevelt had been the leader of America. This man could not stand on his own without help. Yet, he strode his country like a giant through grievous years."

My cousin, Thurm, was assigned to be in charge of the military honor guard to accompany the President's body back to Washington. The hearse rolled past rows of patients at the infantile paralysis foundation. The sound of muffled drums and tolling church bells hung in the air. The procession wound along red dirt roads to the railroad station, where the 11-car presidential train began its journey. Hundreds of thousands of people lined the railroad tracks and stations to get a glimpse of the car carrying the President. The people didn't wave. They wept. Many dropped to their knees and prayed. When night came, the car where the body lay was brilliantly lighted."

The First Lady was riding in the adjoining car on the train. She was concerned about the comfort of the honor guard. She requested sandwiches, doughnuts, and coffee and personally served the men in the other car. Here was a woman known all over the world. She was surrounded by Secret Service protection and trusted staff. She easily could have delegated this simple task.

She asked each man his name and where he was from and thanked each one. Later, she returned with more hot coffee and doughnuts and stayed to visit. It was a class act by a class lady."

I asked, even begged my students to share anecdotes, provocative thoughts, ideas, and quotes with the class and me. I found that they were reluctant to volunteer in class. They didn't want to be branded as brownnosers. They did bring me a multitude of stimulating information that I passed on to my classes. Sometimes they documented these quotes. I couldn't care less who said what. Along with the basic structured core material, I sprinkled my lectures with their interesting contributions. For example:

- Books belong in the home of every person who can't afford hardening of the mental arteries.
- Wouldn't it be nice if people purred?
- Dew is young water.
- A normal person says yes to life.
- The neurotic says yes to life, but the psychotic says no to life.
- If you want to test a man's character, give him power.
- None of us is as smart as all of us.
- Freud said, "The child we once were always resides within us." I paraphrased it: inside every old person is a young person asking, 'what the hell happened?'
- Sex can be compared to a playground slide. Once the child has initiated the slide, there is no way to stop him until he reaches the bottom. Society initiates the slide by letting an individual enter into kissing, hugging, and light petting...which leads to intercourse, the downfall of the slide. Yet society makes sex a little more difficult; they condemn the person who can't stop in the middle of the slide.
- There will always be people who claim our country is going to the dogs. This doesn't mean that everyone should join in the barking.
- I believe in two religions: God and Nature. I understand Nature better. I just don't know whose side God is on.
- Stress on conformity stamps out individuality and interest and encourages apathy.

- We used to have blackboards. Then they became chalkboards. Now they are mounted optical facilitators.
- Those little country schools became rural attendance centers. All gone now. Gobbled up by consolidation.
- Willie Mays' glove is where triples go to die.
- It's easy to be brave at a distance.
- Orchids are grown from seeds so small it takes 30,000 to weigh as much as a grain of wheat.
- It's hard to predict the future because it hasn't happened yet. (Yogi Berra)
- That's a false lie. (Billy Martin)
- Years ago, Thoreau wrote, "Our life is frittered away by detail. Why should we live with such hurry and waste of life? We are determined to be starved before we are hungry."
- If you only have one tool and it's a hammer, you see every problem as a nail.
- A recent thought of mine: I was surprised to see my father's hand protruding from my sleeve. I pointed out the brown liver spots on the back of my hand to our 12-year-old granddaughter. Always the diplomat, she said, "No problem, Grandpa. On you they look good."
- Another thought that hit me personally: In the Valley of the Blind, the one-eyed person is king.
- To illustrate how a teacher can influence a young kid's self-esteem, one student remembered, "I'll never forget my seventh-grade teacher. At that time I was overweight and wore braces on my teeth. Our teacher asked us to turn in a paper on different types of sentences. To demonstrate an exaggeration, I wrote, "I am the most beautiful girl in the world." The teacher wrote back, "This is an exaggeration?"

I have always been intrigued by Indian names. Way back in 1949, I sat in classes with Peter Three Stars. His talent in art made me want to break my fingers. I recorded in my grade book names like Dana Red Earth, Edward Thunder, Patricia Whitehorse, and Angelita Loud Hawk. Names that made Smith and Jones sound rather common.

I debated, but decided I would be remiss without disclosing a secret I have held since 1944. It wasn't fashionable to talk of war experiences after WWII. After all, most able-bodied men served in the war, and no one wanted to be labeled a hero. But as we age over 80 years, and drop by the wayside, we have read Tom Brokaw's books and others that describe WWII.

My dearest friend and buddy in 1943-1944 was a red-haired, fun-loving guy from South Dakota. Women lined up just to dance with him. We spent many nights together in combat. Unbelievable living conditions. Never taking our shoes, socks, clothes off for weeks. We shared awful nights sleeping in one- or two-hour shifts. Whatever we could stand before falling asleep. Then we would shake the other guy awake and it was his turn. On the afternoon of July 31st, we took a hill, a small mountain. It wasn't easy. That afternoon, volunteers were 'asked' to go down below and carry up more grenades and ammo. Jack was one of those appointed. As darkness fell, he was assigned as a BAR assistant to another foxhole. We had always been together. During the night before, on July 30th, I heard music in the distance...music I can't remember or describe...ethereal, not really Oriental. The next morning, I asked our closest foxhole marines if they heard the music. Are you kidding? They looked at me as if I were nuts. I swear, Jack asked me, "Did you hear the music last night?" I was so relieved. "Yes." He stated with conviction, "I know I'm not going to make it through this."

I've never shared this with my K Company family, but if they read this, they will understand.

I write the word 'bravado' on the chalkboard. Before I can turn around, I hear, "False bravery."

"Good. Another comment?" Especially at this moment. Right away, I receive several good examples. I added mine.

"Years ago I was coaching football in an Illinois high school. The boys' locker room was located in the basement of the school. After school, the football players raced down the stairs to suit up for practice. I was a no-nonsense coach that didn't allow people to dilly-dally in the locker room. The boys knew that to dawdle would incur the wrath of God. The locker room was loud, even boisterous at times. I made the common mistake of most high school coaches. Before the first practice of the school year, I insisted that the older boys, and particularly the lettermen, draw the first and best equipment. That left the inferior stuff, the crapola, for the younger smaller new kids. It really should have been the other way around. The little guys needed more protection. On the other hand, why not have the same safe protective equipment for all kids? No money. Yet it seems the United States can come up with billions of dollars for war when education isn't funded? I've been in several small elementary and secondary schools where the libraries are so tiny that students are limited to perhaps 10 or 15 minutes per day. And then they need a pass from a teacher to research a special assignment. Sometimes this also includes an edict that proclaims there will be no browsing in the encyclopedias. No browsing in the encyclopedias is like having no sex in a brothel. But I digress. Back in the football locker room. The assistant coach and student manager tape ankles and knees if needed. Of course, I have our best running back standing on the training table as I personally tape his knee. He is naked as a jaybird. Have you ever seen a naked jaybird? Then, above the din, an awesome silence hits the room. Boys are standing around in various stages of dress and undress. It was unreal. I turned and discovered two senior girls standing at the bottom of the stairs in our locker room. I swear you could have heard the proverbial pin drop.

"Could I help you?" I asked

"The principal asked me to give you this note."

"Did he tell you to bring it down here to our locker room?"

"No. He just said to give this note to you."

I turned to the girl standing beside her. "Grace, what are you doing here?"

"I'm with her," was her only answer.

I could have been the Invisible Man. Both girls never looked at me as they surveyed the room. "Thank you, girls." They disappeared up the stairs. Only then did the silence break. Bravado? The conversations went along the same line:

"Did you see me? I didn't even turn my back."

"I just stood there and looked right at 'em."

"I'll bet they got their eyes full."

Personally, I recall seeing 16-year-old boys holding up towels and even hiding behind locker room doors. Bravado? Remember, this was 1954, before the liberated woman.

It could have been Burns that said, "Oh, to see ourselves as others do." A student added, "If we could see ourselves as others see us, we wouldn't believe it."

Repression is an unconscious tendency to exclude painful thoughts. Suppression is a conscious exclusion of painful desires or thoughts.

When you are born you fit into a cradle three feet long.

When you die you fit into a casket six feet long.

Life in between represents one hell of a fight for a yard.

I visited an elementary school to check on a student teacher. A small boy was sitting in a rocking chair with his back to the class. The chair faced a window where he could stare outside. I asked the teacher, "Has this kid been naughty?"

"Oh, no. That's the Thinking Place. It's sort of a giant King's X. If a child has a special reason or problem, he asks permission to sit there. There is a timer beside it on the windowsill, like one you use when baking cookies. He sets the timer for exactly ten minutes. No one can bother him during this time."

"Do they abuse this privilege? You know, like to goof off every day?"

"Not really. There are some days when no one uses it. They know I trust them."

The Thinking Place. Great creative idea.

One of my students comes into my office.

"Hi, Raymond. Have a chair."

He paces nervously, like a coyote in a zoo. The Viet Nam war is still dragging on and on. He says, "My dad is hounding me to join the army."

"You have a college deferment, don't you?"

"Yes, but my dad says I'm a coward. You were in WWII. What would you do?"

Every fiber, every instinct cries out for me to say, "Don't go, Raymond. Stay in school." Instead, I go Rogerian. "I'm sorry, but I can't answer that. You will have to make this decision for yourself. It could be the most important decision you will ever make. Please forgive me, but it isn't because I don't care."

He came around my desk, put his arm around my shoulders and gave me a little hug. He started toward the door and hesitated. "I really enjoy being in your class. I understand, Mr. Barham. Vaya Con Dios."

Raymond joined the marines. His father was proud of him. In less than a year, Raymond's body was shipped home in a G.I. coffin. His mother still cries. Raymond was a hero. I was the coward.

Dan is standing by the window in my office. His back is toward me. He says, "In class, you said to live alone one must be either a beast or a god. That's heavy stuff."

"I believe Aristotle may have said it first."

"This made me think about how I grew up. You are always telling us stories. Could I tell you one?"

"Of course. You know I love stories."

"I promise this won't take long. I grew up in an orphanage. I don't know how I got there. I have no idea who my parents are. Have you ever been terribly lonely? Have you ever felt like no one in the world really wants you?"

"No, I can't say that, Dan."

"At the orphanage, every Sunday afternoon was visiting day. We sat in our rooms and hoped someone would come to adopt us. I put on my best clothes. When I heard voices or footsteps in the hallway, I sat on the edge of my bed and smiled. I felt like a little puppy in the window of a pet store. Sometimes, when I was real young, people would come into my room and talk to me and then move on. As I grew older, fewer people stopped to visit. They just peeked through the door and walked on by. It didn't take me long to figure out that the people wanted babies or at least very young kids. They also seemed to pick the girls first. I felt like no one in the world would ever want me. I realize now that girls have fewer enuresis problems, fewer stuttering problems, and fewer reading problems. And they are cuter and might create fewer discipline problems down the line. Anyway, I cried myself to sleep many nights. I know for sure that if I ever find someone who wants me, I'll get married and I'll do my very best to see that everyone in our family feels loved and wanted."

A long silence. I didn't speak right away because I didn't trust my voice. I did manage to hold back the tears. The Irish have a problem with emotions. I was proud of myself when my voice didn't croak like a frog. "Danny, right now I can't think of anything that I need more than a hug." We embraced and before I released him I added, "Some day soon, some young lady will be very fortunate to find you, and you won't even know what happened. You are going to be just fine."

Later, a nice young lady did find Dan. He is a highly successful businessman and is very active in his community. Nice guys don't always finish last.

Sights, sounds, smells trigger memories. Every time I hear Willie Nelson or Arlo Guthrie sing the "City of New Orleans" I remember my dad. He was a railroad engineer and two of his trains were the Panama Limited and the City of New Orleans. When I was discharged from the marines, I wasn't 21 and still couldn't vote or buy a beer. My dad received special permission to allow me to ride with him in the cab of his locomotive. Here I was speeding along at 100 miles per hour. The sights, smells, and sounds inside a locomotive are quite different than those inside a comfy club car. I'll never forget that experience. I also vividly recall enjoying steaming hot coffee. And did I detect the coffee being laced with good Irish whiskey? I didn't ask. A fond memory.

A student teacher put this question to her high school history class. "What can you tell me about Harpers Ferry?"

A boy replied, "John Brown must have been some sort of homo. He got into a fight with a guy named Harper. They were fighting over this guy's fairy, and he wasted John Brown." The student teacher said the class seemed to buy this answer, until it was discovered that Harpers Ferry was a town in northeastern West Virginia.

Our senses are wonderful gifts that we sometimes take for granted. The three months when I was totally blind taught me to appreciate my vision when it was regained. A blind person misses the beauty of a sunrise or sunset. A blind woman misses the excitement and the fun of shopping for clothes if she can't mix or match colors. How do you describe the breathtaking colors of a rooster pheasant, a wood duck, an indigo bunting? Degrees of color blindness are passed on through mothers to their sons. A dirty trick of nature.

People who can't hear miss the effect of laughter, which is good for the soul. Laughter is contagious. We should start an epidemic. Who can suppress a smile at the sound of a giggle coming from a baby or a small child? What is it like to never hear the wonderful sound of music? What if you could never hear the magic sound of a robin singing after a spring rain?

Nothing elicits nostalgia more than smells. Most of the things I have enjoyed in life really and truly are free. I remember the smell and atmosphere of the old railroad depots like the Chicago Illinois Central Station, Penn Station, Grand Central Station, and Union Station. I love the smell of wood smoke from a cabin, pine trees when it's raining, fresh-cut alfalfa hay, a new box of Crayolas on the first day of school, fresh bread from the oven, soft warm puppies, hot coffee in a duck blind, the new car smell (until someone lights a cigar in it), popcorn at a ballgame, leather, or a freshly bathed baby.

I don't think it would be asking too much to at least briefly expose young kids to some of the longest Broad way runs. So they might miss a couple of days of logarithm tables? Would it mess up their little minds to recognize some music or lines from plays such as...?
- Fiddler on the Roof
- Life with Father
- Tobacco Road
- Hello Dolly
- My Fair Lady
- Man of La Mancha
- Abie's Irish Rose
- Oklahoma
- Harvey
- Hair

Going back to the 1950's, I was teaching and coaching at Rhinelander High School. Of all the high schools I taught in and later supervised student teachers, I feel this was an exceptional faculty. Our English department was great. Miss Benson was well versed and knew her subject well. Unfortunately, she seemed to hate kids. The students always tried to avoid her classes. She had been there for years. She had been left a fortune by her grandfather and father. The school board had to remind her to cash her monthly check, which she stashed in a drawer somewhere. She didn't need the money. She didn't like boys, but she loathed girls. Each fall, a new group of kids got stuck in 'Old Lady Benson's' classes. I'm not saying they didn't learn English, they did. It simply wasn't pleasant. She treated her students as if they were all cretins. After we had built a beautiful new high school, the girls' bathroom was not near Miss Benson's classroom down the hall. One day Miss Benson came out of the girls' room with her skirt caught in her girdle, exposing her derriere. Between classes, this news spread like a prairie fire. "Have you heard about 'Old Lady Benson'?"

At this point I should mention that I was also the track coach. We were the most northern located school in the conference in a northern state not noted for track stars. When I reported for the track season as coach, I found we had nine dedicated track kids from the previous year. I persuaded (conned) 50 boys out for the squad. I soon discovered a sprinter who had never been out for track. No one in those days had heard of 'all weather' tracks. So, since we were the northernmost and coldest with the latest track practices, I decided to practice in the hallways of our big new school. Hey, I'm the track coach, and it is snowing outside. After school (4:00 p.m.), and without permission from Mr. Evans, the principal, I start my sprinters and a high hurdler (one hurdle) down the vast hallway of our new school. It is freezing ice and snow outdoors. The hallway is deserted. Perfect. My hurdler and two sprinters are flying flat-out, three abreast, when 'Old Lady Benson' backs out of her room and reaches to close the door. I didn't think she knew what hit her. Papers flew into the air and then slowly drifted down to the floor. My tracksters never hesitated. They escaped up the down staircase. I was terrified. This woman personified, was the epitome of every math teacher that I had endured and survived in my youth. I walked backwards and hid in the entrance of another classroom. I waited to see if she could make it on her own.

When I was a small lad, my dad told me, "You can kill a snake by cutting off its head, but it doesn't really die until the sun goes down. That's why the tail continues to wiggle."

Old Lady Benson was tough. I watched as she picked up her papers and limped out of sight. She had a unique walking style. I recalled the students describing her as waddling down the hall with her skirt hem caught her girdle.

The next morning there was a note in my mailbox. "See Mr. Evans before class."

I walked into his office. "Close the door." Bad sign. "Have a chair." Not good. "Wayne, you are a good teacher, a good coach." He is buttering me up. He continued, "I believe you are a born aberrant. Things that you do seem to turn into aberrations." I wasn't familiar with the term. Never heard of 'aberrations', but it didn't sound good. I wasn't going to plead guilty until I was charged.

Mr. Evans asked politely, "Did you have permission to run your track team through the halls of our new school? Did you ask the superintendent, the school board, the custodians, if it would be okay? You certainly didn't check with me." He knows. How does this man do this?

"My Gawd, Coach...Miss Benson, of all people!"

Before I could answer, he admitted, "The walleye season opens in the morning. I suppose you and your friend, Todd McEldowny will be going together. I don't suppose you would let me tag along? I realize that you don't want to associate with me. It's a bit lonely at the top."

It was so nice, so comfortable, so appreciated to teach in a school system at any level where the teachers respected their superiors.

"Hey, we would love to have you join us."

"Can I guess where we are going in the morning?"

"Sure, I love games."

"Oneida, Crescent, Squash, Black Lake, Big Twin, Butternut, Lake Tomahawk?"

I assured him these were good choices, but we were going to hit the Rainbow Flowage on the Wisconsin River at sunrise. He was as pleased as a little kid blowing out candles on a birthday cake. He offered, "I'll bring a bucketful of the best silver shiners and golden shiners I can find in town."

I brought a big thermos of coffee and a bottle of blackberry brandy. McEldowny's wife sent along a huge sack full of sandwiches. Inside the big sack, the sandwiches were divided so that Evans and I split two-thirds of them, and the other third was for her husband. Reason? When we got into the sandwiches, Todd unwrapped his and read a small note, sort of like a fortune cookie. Evans and I had no notes. I couldn't stand it. I snatched a note that read, "Love you, honey." Another read, "Good luck. Have fun." A third said, "Guess what's waiting for you at home?"

We killed 'em on the Rainbow Flowage.

In the mid 1950's, the walleye opener in mid-May rivaled the Milwaukee Braves baseball champions and the Green Bay Packer dynasty. These were the glory days of Wisconsin sports. It was simply nuts. People stayed up late or all night on Friday evening to party and get ready for Saturday morning. People bought fishing licenses and braved wind, rain, and many times snow to fish on opening day. Many of these people never fished again during the rest of the spring, summer, and fall. It was a ritual, a tradition.

Eight of us started an annual affair that lasted for nearly 50 years. We formed a group that rented two cabins on a different lake each year for the walleye opening. A two-day fishing trip. Of course, we had Manhattans, food, and poker at night. All of the lakes within 20 miles of town were full of big fat hungry walleyes in the 1950's. We each tossed in a dollar for the winner of the biggest fish. At dusk, I hooked a beautiful 7-pound walleye that my partner skillfully netted. Caught it on a yellow jig. Todd and I came in as darkness fell. The rest of the guys were preparing supper. We walked in and I held up my prize and said proudly, "You want to pay me now or later?"

Ben Murphy said, "Put it on the porch with the others. You got third place."

In the darkness, we had walked past the other fish on the floor of the porch. Here was a 9-pounder, and a 10-pounder. These would be unheard-of wall hangers today. We routinely ate them in those days.

After supper, the poker game began. Not big stakes, but Todd and I each lost about five dollars. In the 1950's this was a lot of money for a teacher. On our way home Sunday evening I told Todd, "Dorothy will kill me when she finds out I lost five dollars. My kids both need snow boots for this winter." I still live with the guilt.

One of the regulars of our original group of eight was an insurance company millionaire. Nice guy. Six of the guys had modest small boats and motors. He had a huge Cris Craft complete with a small bar. Todd and I rented a dinghy and rowed around the lake. Once on Lake Tomahawk, the weather was especially cruel. Rain, snow, and high winds kept us off the lake. Our rich friend had his boat moored to the dock. It broke loose and was floating downwind along the shore. Don't ask me why, but I raced out of the cabin, dived into the icy water, swam out and grabbed the broken line, and towed the boat back to shore. A stupid thing to do, but it was one of the things that the group brought up in conversation for many years on each fishing trip. A macho thing. Dumb.

Every five years, South Dakota elementary and secondary teachers are required to pick up a few college credit hours to renew their teaching certificates. They do this by taking on-campus courses, summer school offerings, or extension classes. I taught a 7:00 a.m. summer school on-campus class. I had perhaps 20 students, mostly older women already teaching, with a sprinkling of younger students in my summer class. I lived four blocks from my room in Main Hall. I was never late. Seldom early. I walked into my classroom ready to go at 7:00 a.m. sharp. One morning I was two or three minutes late. I apologized to the class and said lamely, "I suppose I had better start my morning walk up here a bit earlier." There was a distinct snickering from the left corner of the room. A hand went up. "Mr. Barham, we commute to and from Burke for this class. It's 85 miles from here." I'm embarrassed. These women weren't through with me. A voice from the other corner of the room exclaimed, "We can beat that. We commute every morning from Wessington Springs—115 miles." They were never late for class. After that, neither was I.

I taught an extension class in Reliance, South Dakota. We met in the high school in this small West River town every Tuesday evening at 7:00 p.m. for twelve weeks. It was a long 135-mile drive, but I enjoyed it. There were 25 women in the class. Most of them had been teaching for several years in rural schools. Many of them were still trying to pick up enough credits to complete a degree. They never missed a class. They were never late.

They always had done their homework. They also brought sandwiches, cookies, bars, coffee, tea, and other treats. We had a 20-minute break that turned out to be a social hour. All the ladies knew each other. I was the only man present. A delightful experience for me. During the break of our second meeting, I discovered that one of these women lived on a farm just outside of Kimball. She drove from Kimball to Reliance after supper on Tuesday evenings. A distance of 35 miles. Since I drove right past Kimball on my way to Reliance, it seemed only logical that she could ride with me. I offered to stop at the huge truck stop and café in Kimball where I usually bought gas anyway. She could drive her car and leave it at the truck stop. Then I could drop her off there after class on my way home. The weather could turn ugly very quickly during a South Dakota winter. Our class wasn't over until 10:00 p.m. I didn't like the idea of a woman being out on the highway late at night in bad weather, if it could be avoided. She hesitated, as if mulling it over.

"For crying out loud, Betty, what's there to think about?" a woman asked.

"What's your problem?" asked another.

"It only makes sense."

"Go for it."

"How do you think the rest of us get home?" Laughter.

With the encouragement of her peers, Betty agreed. "But I insist on paying you whatever you think it's worth. At least for the gas."

"Hey, I'm driving a state-owned car and use a college credit card for the gas. I couldn't charge you for something that doesn't cost me a cent. In fact, I might be bending the rules a bit by having you ride along with me in a school car. You know, insurance or lawsuits? Who cares? Next Tuesday, I'll pick you up at the truck stop."

For the next ten weeks, everything went smoothly. In our last class meeting, right after our break, the custodian came into our room and advised me to cut the class early. It was beginning to snow, and the wind was picking up. Wind, the curse of the Dakotas. I was in the process of handing out the papers for the final exam. I told these prairie women what I had just been informed. I wasn't a bit surprised when they all agreed to finish the test. They had driven in snow before. And this was before 4x4 pickups; SUV's were not yet fashionable.

It took longer than usual to drive from Reliance to Kimball. The snowflakes that I saw blowing across the road in front of me must have landed in another county. The windshield wipers were almost mesmerizing. After nearly three months, I had learned that Betty was known as an excellent teacher. I learned this, not from her, but from her peers. I also knew that she lived on a very small farm, and her husband had been injured in a farm accident and was handicapped. All this, too, from her peers. Our rides together were relatively quiet. She wasn't prone to prattle.

The bright headlights on my car were useless. I drove slowly with the dimmer switch on. I was surprised and relieved when Betty spoke. "Have I told you about my thirteen-year-old daughter?"

"No."

"This morning I was up early, and she also got up early. She said, 'Mama, I'm not complaining, but wouldn't it be great if we just had water inside the house? Just think what it would be like to turn a faucet and get hot water. I wouldn't have to go out to the well to bring the water in and heat it on the stove to do the dishes.'"

I didn't know what to say. Rather than say something dumb, I didn't respond. In the silence that followed, I knew she was crying. In the darkness, I couldn't see the tears. Hell, she was sitting on my blind side, thanks to the Japanese. Were these tears of contentment, frustration, love? Who knows what makes a woman cry? I was still wrapping my little mind around what she had said, when she added, "I love her so much. I don't know what I would do without her." I believe this answered my question about the tears. Nat King Cole sang in one of his biggest hits:

The greatest thing, you'll ever learn
Is just to love,
And be loved in return.

When we reached the truck stop in Kimball, the snow had abated. I was thinking of things to say to this woman. I admired her greatly. I didn't want to terminate a three-month friendship with a stupid goodbye.

She possibly read my thoughts. I could see that she, like most women, was way ahead of me.

"Wait here. I have something for you."

I parked behind her car so that my headlights illuminated the area. She got out of my car and walked over to her own. She lifted the lid on the trunk of her car and hefted a rather heavy package. She walked gingerly on the ice back to my car and handed this package through the window. "I knew you would not take money. So I got up early this morning and killed and dressed this turkey for you before I went to my schoolhouse. I enjoyed the class, and it was nice to visit with all those women every Tuesday. I looked forward to it. Thank you so much for everything."

For once, I had an appropriate thought. "I'll put this turkey in the freezer, and we will have it for our Christmas dinner."

"That would be nice."

Goodbyes have never been easy for me. Especially with a woman. I'm destined, it seems, to be left in awe. So, instead of saying something, I reached out to give her a hug, but she was gone. A remarkable woman. A perfect example of an androgynous person. Strong, tough, resilient, but still feminine. Nothing more interesting and fascinating than the feminine mystique.

I waited to make sure her car started. Then I watched as the taillights disappeared into the softly falling snow. A potential South Dakota blizzard had blessedly fizzled. I had seen the winters of 1948, 1949, and 1950 and respected and appreciated what twelve-foot snowdrifts can do. Nothing is more humbling than the power of Mother Nature, Mother Earth.

Shortly after I was married in 1948, I committed a serious faux pas. You'll recall that I made an innocent remark about the difference between my beautiful young bride's potato soup and my mother's. This one little innocent remark resulted in me making my own potato soup for the rest of my life. I used this story in class to lead into a piece of advice for young men: Do not praise another woman too lavishly in the presence of your wife, your mother, or, for that matter, any other woman. Too bad I'm not smart enough to heed my own advice.

Last summer, we were invited to a sit-down dinner…in a home, mind you. Entertaining in the home instead of eating out has become passé. Sort of like the lost art of letter writing. Our host and hostess were very gracious. Here were four couples that had been friends for many years. After a relaxing cocktail hour, we were summoned to the table in the formal dining room. Part of the demise of the sit-down dinner can be blamed on having a dining room deleted from modern homes. So here we are, Mark and Donna at each end of the dining room table. In between are seated Wayne and Dorothy, Paul and Florence, and Todd and Georgia. The Irish in me must heighten my emotions. I was touched as we lifted our wine glasses in a toast to our host. At our age, it is so easy to become nostalgic. What does a young person know of nostalgia? I began with a sincere compliment. "What a wonderful evening. What a beautiful table set for old friends." I should have left it at that. I'm sure everyone agreed. But no, I rambled on, "Look at this. I have never seen so many dishes. Saucers for the coffee. A small plate under the soup. A special small plate for dinner rolls. And little individual salt and pepper shakers." I extolled everything in sight. Of course, Donna beamed and our host was proud. I was still babbling when I crossed the line and said, "I have never seen a more beautiful dinner." My wife kicked me under the table and whispered, "Shut up and eat."

A few days later, we were invited to the McEldowny's for dinner. Todd and Georgia had been present when I heaped all the praise on Donna at our super dinner a few evenings prior. This time there would be the four of us. Two very close couples. After the usual Wisconsin Happy Hour, we were ushered into the dining room. It was a candlelit atmosphere. The first thing that I noticed was that Georgia designated, "Wayne, you sit there opposite Todd at the other end of the table." In the dim light, I saw newspapers spread under my chair. The rest of the table was absolutely elegant. These three people were treated like royalty. Linen napkins, the finest china plates, sterling silver everywhere, fluted wine glasses, and yes, even crystal individual salt and pepper shakers. I was seated in a different mode. I stared at a paper towel for a napkin. I had a heavy-duty non-leak paper plate, a paper cup for a wine glass, and plastic knives, forks and spoons. The final touch was a can of pepper and a big box of Morton's salt right off the kitchen shelf. This genteel woman made her point. Will I ever learn?

Getting paid for teaching psychology is like stealing. It is so interesting and so much fun. My goal was to introduce topics that would stimulate introspection. The students really got involved and contributed to mnemonics. We would first define it, and anything close was fine. We were simply looking for ways to improve or develop memory. Like a formula or a rhyme to help remember.

Thirty days hath September, April, June and November.

Geography: George Edward's old grandma rode a pig home yesterday.

Mississippi: M-i-crooked letter-crooked letter-i-crooked letter-crooked letter-i-humpback-humpback-i.

There was always something about counting across and in between the knuckles.

The way they organized notes and material to study for a test.

Even the most quiet and shy students got involved and offered their ideas and personal little tricks. Hey, anything that works! Time was the only factor that forced me to move on to another subject. I still can't believe the creative methods these young people came up with to help them, especially with their short-term memory. My personal reward came from having them—piqued by curiosity—discover ideas, thoughts that they could actually use in life. There should be pragmatism even in the fun courses of college life.

If there is such a thing as a disparity in life, I offer the fact that mothers, through their genes, pass on in various degrees to their sons, color blindness. How many women have you ever known that are afflicted with color blindness?

Women seem to be tuned into color more than men. I asked my male students to list all of the colors they could come up with, and I gave them a short time frame. They always hit the primary colors and usually included green and brown. With men, black is black and white is white. Women will spend hours matching blacks and whites. With men, who cares? Beige is an example. It's a variable color even among women. They might say it is sort of light grayish, yellowish, brown. They describe burgundy as dark purplish, reddish brown. Don't even ask men to describe taupe. Most guys have never heard of it.

Here are some of the colors women have to choose from while shopping: burgundy, leather, gray, ruby, bark, stone, charcoal, dusty lilac, blue steel, taupe, ivory, cream, camel, double espresso, raspberry, antique beige, watermelon, bright pool, wild grape, smoky blue, nude, pearl, petrol, fuchsia, flamingo pink, French blue, olive, winter blue, mahogany, rust, pecan, loden, gingerbread, currant, ivy, teal, champagne, mushroom, indigo, kiwi, amethyst, wheat, caramel, chambray, and turquoise. Did I forget cinnamon and plum? There are others.

A departed friend of mine was an admired school superintendent. He was a nice guy. He was also colorblind. His charming wife made sure that his socks were in perfect pairs in his dresser drawer. He had no problem with socks that had designs on them. Socks of plain solid colors were a challenge. She rolled these in pairs. Sometimes after a mild argument or quarrel, this mild-mannered and sweet lady rolled two different colored socks together. His friends and co-workers could tell how things were going at home for Bob.

One last piece of advice I passed along to my male students: Believe it or not, one of the first things that a woman notices about a man is his shoes. I know a man that is actually known for his vast wardrobe. He is impeccably dressed. However, he never shines his shoes. I mentioned this to him and he growled, "I own the most expensive shoes that money can buy. I don't have time to shine 'em." Wrong. And don't forget to shine the edges of the soles. Check out any U.S. Marine on liberty. No matter what uniform he is wearing—blues, greens, or khakis, his shoes will sparkle. If not, he will be in a heap of trouble.

I believe it was George Gobel who said, "Sometimes I feel like the world is a tuxedo, and I'm a pair of brown shoes."

PART SEVEN

Dogs

Scarlet

My dad had twelve brothers and sisters. I loved all my aunts and uncles. My mother had five siblings. I loved all of them. My dad's brother, Dewey ("Dude"), was not one of my mother's favorites. Perhaps it was because he spent a lot of time in the field with his hunting dogs. Or maybe he tipped a few drinks? Hey, he was a typical Irish railroad engineer. I was into the outdoors—hunting and fishing before I can remember. My dad took me hunting with him before I entered school. I walked the fields with him until I was exhausted, and then he and my uncles took turns carrying me on their backs. I could look over their shoulders and sight down a shotgun as they aimed at flushing pheasants and quail.

It was in the 1930's, and I rode my one-pedal bicycle to junior high school. Uncle Dude lived just three blocks west of us. I frequently stopped off to visit with him when he wasn't working. People in those days spent much of their time in the front porch swing. A seemingly lost treasure today.

Uncle Dude had a beautiful female Irish setter. He surprised me with, "Trixie is going to have pups; they are purebred Irish setters. I'll sell them, but I'm going to give you one. You can have first choice, the pick of the litter. I won't let them go until they are six weeks old. Can you keep a secret? You can surprise your folks then."

I was thrilled. Here I am the anointed one. What an honor. The pups were born. I never missed a day without visiting the pen behind Uncle Dude's house. As they grew, it became easy to pick out the biggest, the strongest, the little guys. Their faces were different, even to a human. Then I noticed this female that sat alone in the corner of the pen. She seemed to avoid the roughhousing that went on. I could reach down over the pen and pick each pup up. Every time I picked up this female with the soulful eyes, she snuggled into my hands and when I held her close enough, she licked my face. No contest. This one was mine. Uncle Dude was pleased with my choice. "Most people want a male. The females are the last to go."

Six weeks passed. I rode Popeye, my bike, to get my pup. I had given this a lot of thought and decided to call her Scarlet. A perfect fit. I picked her up and got on my bike. The sun glistened on her red coat. I cradled her in my arm against my chest. I could feel her tail wagging. Which one of us was most happy?

I opened the back door of our house. My mother was always in the kitchen. "Look what I've got, Mom. Uncle Dude gave her to me. Isn't she beautiful? I'll take care of her and train her."

I can't explain the expression on my mother's face. I can't begin to describe it, but I have never forgotten that look. Perhaps surprise? But no reaction at all.

I took Scarlet to the basement. The basement had a cement ledge that ran along two sides. A two-burner gas plate sat on the south ledge. My mother boiled clothes in a copper boiler and stirred them with a stick. We took our Saturday night bath in a regular washtub that sat on the floor in front of the furnace. The only bathroom was a closet-sized cubicle that my dad had enclosed for privacy. I was sitting on the throne while Scarlet was exploring her new surroundings. Suddenly the door flew open. It was right out of Alfred Hitchcock's movie, "Psycho", when Anthony Perkins ripped the shower curtain open and stabbed Janet Leigh. My mother stood over me and was flailing away with her stirring stick. I was caught with my pants down. I held up my hands and arms to ward off the blows. I was big and strong enough to finally grab both of her wrists. She was exhausted and breathed heavily. "You didn't ask permission to bring that dog home. This is my home. Don't you ever go over my head again. Now you march right out of here and take this dog back to your Uncle Dewey."

I held back the tears when I put Scarlet back in the pen with the rest of the pups. As I turned to leave, she followed me along the fence, and when she came to the end and could go no farther, she stood on her hind legs, held on to the fence, and whined.

Uncle Dude's voice startled me. He had watched as I kissed the top of her head and placed her gently inside the pen. "What's wrong?"

I related my plight. He told me he would see that she got a good home. He also made me feel a bit better by saying, "It's okay, Son. We don't want to cause any hard feelings. This too shall pass. Some day you will forget all about this."

My mother died when she was 97. At the funeral, my mind raced from one scene to another. Like clicking the remote of the TV. All the wonderful memories flew by as I remembered a good and loving mother. But tucked away and not forgotten after all those years, I recalled taking that beautiful puppy back to Uncle Dude. It broke my heart. My mother was using Tough Love before psychologists invented the term. I never forgave her.

Chips

Mayne Talsma's closest neighbor lived a mile and a half away. Mayne's huge ranch sprawled along the Missouri River. I considered him my best friend. He was a bachelor and the best outdoorsman I ever knew. He was partial to Labradors when it came to hunting dogs. He got his Labs from a nationally known character named Mayo Kellogg in Madison, South Dakota. Chips was one of these purebred females. Mayne had never seen a stray dog on his ranch, but when his pride and joy, Chips, was obviously 'with child', he could only surmise it was an Immaculate Conception.

When the seven tiny mongrel pups were born, he drove at least a half-mile out of sight from his house where he killed and buried them.

As a typical cowboy, he had several pairs of fancy boots that would fit all occasions. He also owned one old pair that he called his everyday work boots. They were worn, comfortable, and his favorites. They were always muddy, dirty, and prone to be left on the porch. Upon rising one morning, he went out on the porch to discover one of his boots was missing. He searched everywhere. Never found it. He finally concluded that this was some sort of joke that a friend had pulled and after a period of time, this person wouldn't be able to keep silent any longer and would produce the boot. It never happened, but he kept the one boot just in case.

Weeks passed. Mayne was going to take a routine check on his cattle, so he invited Chips to ride along with him in his Jeep. She loved riding in the Jeep. By accident, he drove near the site where he had buried the pups. Chips leaped from the Jeep while it was still moving and ran to the grave. She stood there sniffing the earth. He walked over to Chips. She looked up at him with those big brown eyes as if to say, "I know what you did." He also discovered his missing boot placed on the grave. He felt guilty. He felt awful, but you simply can't unhappen a happening. He picked up his boot and walked to the Jeep. Chips walked beside him with tail and ears drooping. He was about to toss the boot into the back of the jeep, when he thought, "What the hell, she carried that boot all the way out here and placed it right on this spot." So he takes it back and places it on the grave. Then he looks around and finds a big stone, which he puts next to the boot to mark the grave. Now he returns to the Jeep with Chips leaping and bounding all around him with tail and ears held high. She had watched all this intently. Now she was happily wagging her powerful tail. He had assuaged his conscience.

Dogs are loyal. Dogs are forgiving.

Daisy

Years ago, an old man lived in a ramshackle house at the edge of town. When he died, he left an old yellow Labrador mourning on the front porch. She waited for him to come home, but this wasn't going to happen. People noticed this old dog, but no one wanted a gray-faced Labrador. Besides, it was during the days of the Great Depression. Times were tough. After a few days, the town cop, Cecil, took her some table scraps and water. Someone had told him her name was Daisy. A few people suggested he "take her out and shoot her." Or "Why don't you just put her out of her misery?"

More days passed. Nothing had changed. Cecil decided that perhaps he would be doing the right thing by destroying the old dog. He had to coax her into his car with a few pieces of cornbread. She was starving. He headed out of town trying to choose a place where no one would see or hear him when the deed was done. Daisy moved over and sat close beside him, put her head next to his shoulder, and looked at him with soulful eyes. "Damn." His mind raced. A nice old couple, Lars and Hilda Johnson, lived in the little community of Running Water. It was stretching things to call it a town. Nestled on the Missouri River, it was the end of the line for the railroad. It was known mainly for its bootleg whisky, beer, and dances. Several Catholic families lived there. The Johnsons had a lane that ran a hundred yards from the gravel road to their house. It was noon and they were having lunch. Lars came outside and asked, "What brings you here, Cecil?"

"Oh, I just happened to be going by and thought I would ask you if the catfish are biting now."

Mrs. Johnson opened the door and scolded Lars, "Why don't you ask Cecil in for lunch?"

"No thanks," Cecil lied, "I have to get back to town." Lars looked in to the car and spied Daisy.

"I didn't know you had a dog."

"It's not mine." He opened the door and Daisy jumped out and sat beside him. "No one wants her so I'm going to have to shoot her. Seems like such a nice old dog, though."

Hilda heard this. "She looks starved. Let me get her something." The something turned out to be a small chunk of home-cured ham. Daisy took it gently from Hilda's fingers. Then the Labrador magic began to work. The powerful happy tail thwacker and those pleading eyes. Bingo. Cecil knew he was off the hook. He even felt a bit smug.

Hilda asked, "What's her name?"

"Daisy."

Hilda looked at her husband. "This is our dog. Come on, Daisy." They disappeared into the house.

Lars looked at Cecil and smiled. Cecil winked in return. Lars looked at the back door, then looked again at Cecil and shrugged his shoulders. He knew he had been had. Cecil offered his hand. The handshake was firm and long.

"Thanks, Lars."

The Johnsons had a small farm near Running Water. Their closest neighbors were George Rush, Sr., his wife Ann, and their son, George Rush, Jr. The old man was a left-handed card player that no one trusted. Junior was a clone of his father. He had beady little eyes set close together. He could have passed for Cyclops, the one-eyed Titan that forged thunderbolts for Zeus. Junior had the reputation of trouble—a liar and a thief, but never convicted. Local people thought that much nicer kids were in reform school.

Winter passed and spring arrived to melt the South Dakota snow. Lars was checking his fence that bordered the Rush's land. He spied Junior digging a hole along the fence line. As Lars approached, he discovered that Junior had found a coyote den and had dug out the pups and killed them with the shovel.

"Dad will be glad to know I killed all these coyotes," he beamed proudly.

Lars didn't answer and turned to leave when a faint sound came from back in the hole—a short whine or cry. Junior heard it too. He started digging again and soon a little gray furry pup was exposed. Junior raised the shovel to smash the pup's head as he had done to the others.

"Wait!" Lars stopped him. "I'll give you fifty cents. Don't kill it."

Junior was skeptical. "You got the money with you?"

Lars reached into his pocket and produced the fifty-cent coin. They made coins like that back in those days. He reached down and picked up the tiny fur ball and put it inside his coat. On his way to the house, he wondered how he would explain all this to Hilda. He decided not to mention the fifty cents.

He entered the house, took off his coat, and held this furry little creature in his huge hands. "Look what I've got, Hilda."

She turned and spied the pup. "What in the world is that?"

"It's a baby coyote. Junior Rush killed the rest of the litter." He handed it to her. She smelled it, stroked it. It was so soft, so helpless. She cradled it high on her bosom. It snuggled close to her and reached up and licked her chin. Good move. "Oh, well, we have the cow, so milk won't be a problem. I'll have to bottle feed it until it can drink from a saucer. We can make a little bed for it."

Daisy was watching this scene unfold. Hilda put the pup on the floor. It was clumsy. Could barely stand and walk. Like an awkward toddler. Daisy circled this strange creature. She sniffed it and turned it over on its back with her nose. More sniffing head to tail.

It was decided to leave the pup's bed in the kitchen that night. Early spring nights can become very cold. Upon arising the next morning, Hilda found Daisy lying next to the pup's bed, but the pup had managed to tumble out of the low bed onto the floor and was nestled happily and comfortably next to Daisy, the surrogate mother. The baby coyote tried to nurse from Daisy, but of course, this was impossible. A few deep growls straightened out this situation. As the pup grew, it became a bit more agile. It crawled over Daisy, pouncing on her tail, until the old dog would tire of this, and that deep growl ended the play. The pup then retreated a few steps, sat and stared at Daisy…then slowly crawled forward, invaded her space, pressed his luck and licked her on the nose and snout. It was sort of an apology. But then after being chastised, the romping would begin again. The old dog was very tolerant.

As the coyote matured, Hilda decided it should have a name. What sort of name is appropriate for a little male coyote? It was something to ponder. Lars exclaimed, "You know something interesting? That little 'snootlicker' still ambles up to Daisy and licks her nose when he wants to make up to her if he has been bad."

"That's it!"
"That's what?"
"Let's call him little Snootlicker."

Daisy and Snootlicker became inseparable. He was indeed her shadow. They lived outside most of the time. They slept under the porch or under a huge lilac bush. They dug holes to keep warm or cool as need be.

The word was spread that the Johnsons had a pet coyote. Very few people actually got a glimpse of it. Snootlicker was very wary of people, and he was a master at hiding. Those few that did see him thought he only had one eye, because he was usually peeking around the corner of the house or from behind a tree. When he heard a wagon or car turn off the main gravel road and start up the lane to the house, he simply vanished.

Old John McFarland came to Running Water twice each month. His horse-drawn wagon always held a pile of empty burlap bags when he arrived. When he left town, these same gunnysacks had something in them. He really wasn't fooling anyone. No one talked about the stills that operated along the Missouri River back in the woods and ravines. Moonshiners made excellent white lightning. They used corn, rye, or barley for mash. Mind you now, it was only a rumor. No one knew for sure who these nefarious men were. No one knew where the stills were located. But everyone knew where and from whom you could buy the stuff. Among the names that were mentioned, if you had suitable references, were Pat McGregor, Tim O'Brien, Mike McLaury, and Joe Flannery. Sort of an ethnic thing.

When old John McFarland passed by the Johnson's lane, his big mongrel dog was either riding in the wagon or trotting alongside in the road. Whenever he spied old Daisy somewhere in the yard, he bolted up the lane and beat the hell out of her. He was younger and stronger, and she was an old, weak victim. As a pup and young coyote, Snootlicker would go to Daisy and comfort her. He licked her wounds if any blood was visible. And then he licked her nose as if to kiss her.

Weeks turned into months. It was one of those hot July days when the sun seemed determined to cremate the earth. No air-conditioning, and many homes had no electricity to enjoy the comfort of a fan. Just open the windows and hope for a breeze. Snootlicker is now a full-grown adult. He is all muscle and bone.

He hears a wagon approaching along the gravel road. As always, he hides under the lilac bush.

Daisy has just gone to the well where the Johnsons kept a pail of water by the pump for their pets. The wagon turns out to hold John McFarland. His dog is eagerly scanning the yard for Daisy. She is caught in the open. The dog races up the lane. This time he never reaches his prey. A gray streak shoots from under the lilac bush with the speed of a hissing arrow. This surprise attack knocks the dog off his feet. He is confronted by a mouthful of snarling, slashing, glistening fangs and teeth. All the pent-up anger and frustration is alleviated. This cur manages to free himself and flees for his life back down the lane. Snootlicker in hot pursuit. The dog howls in pain as his legs are being nipped from behind. One last chomp on the hamstring as they near the mailbox by the road. Snootlicker returns to Daisy and—even though out of breath and panting heavily—he licks her old gray face vigorously. It was over. After that, when John McFarland came to town, his dog stayed in the wagon or made a wide circle in the field opposite the lane. He also walked with a distinct limp after that encounter.

My good friend, Mayne Talsma, related this story to me. It was a cold miserable South Dakota day. I never saw him drink a cup of coffee. He liked tea or whisky. He also knew that the Johnsons were tea drinkers, and Hilda always had fresh-baked cookies to serve. He turned into their lane as the 20 M.P.H. winds were already forming pillow drifts across the road. As he was welcomed into their house, he noticed old Daisy snoozing behind the stove and he saw the coyote disappear into another room. Soon they were sitting at the big kitchen table. Hilda had steaming teacups on saucers for the three of them. Also there was a sugar bowl and a platter of cookies. Lars said, "Watch this, Mayne." He called, "Come here, Snootlicker." In a fraction of a second, the coyote was sitting on the floor next to Lars. Mayne had never been this close to him before. Lars took a cookie from the platter and held it in his fingertips above the table. The coyote never wavered. Just sat there and concentrated on the cookie. Lars said, "Okay!" It happened so fast Mayne couldn't believe it. Snootlicker was a gray blur as he leaped high into the air and gently snatched the cookie, came down on the table and disappeared into another room. Nothing was disturbed on the table. What a performance.

My friend was so impressed. He suggested that they get a bright-colored collar for their pet. Most farmers and ranchers shot coyotes whenever they could. So Lars found a red harness that fit Snootlicker. When he put it on him, Daisy was watching. What goes through a dog's mind? Did she think Snootlicker was being punished by having to wear this? Was this a special gift that she didn't deserve to have? And also, what was he thinking? Was he being punished or rewarded? Anyway, it was a very good idea. The red harness could easily be seen at 200 yards through the scope of a 30.06 or .270 rifle. Better safe than sorry.

A few weeks passed. After breakfast, Lars went outside to do some chores. He soon noticed that Daisy was alone in the yard. Snootlicker was nowhere to be seen. Lars called. Nothing. The coyote was gone. He had never left the yard before. Very unusual. Lars went back into the house to inform Hilda. They talked about all of the possibilities and decided that he might have answered the call of the wild. It was very common to hear coyotes yipping and howling from the hilltops above the river at night. As much as he would be missed, they consoled themselves with the idea that after all, he is a wild animal and is back with his kind. Daisy didn't seem to agree. She didn't eat, and she moped around as if missing her friend.

Another day passed. Then on the third day, Snootlicker was back again. He teased Daisy by leaping over her, pouncing, racing around her. It was heartwarming to see them together again.

Nearly a month passed, and Snootlicker was gone again. This time the Johnsons were philosophical. He will probably show up again, and if not, he is with his kind. They could live with this.

Hilda loves to cook. She is up early. Gorgeous sunrise over the Missouri River. She has the coffee on the stove and is thinking of pancakes and sausage for breakfast. She gazes out over the river then down the lane to the mailbox. She is surprised to see Daisy by the road. That's a long walk for an old dog that suffers from arthritis in her joints. The vet had advised them to give her half an aspirin twice each day to help her endure the pain. So it was a long, stiff-legged walk for her to the road. Hilda calls her, but she doesn't come. Lars comes stumbling into the kitchen for his morning coffee. Hilda says, "I can see Daisy down by the mailbox, but she won't come when I call her."

"You know how deaf she is getting. She probably can't hear you. I'll go see."

As he approached Daisy, he saw that there was an object beside her. She was lying with her head on her front paws. The object turned out to be the carcass of an animal. It had been expertly skinned from nose to the tip of the tail. A red harness had been tossed beside the animal, as if to say 'this wasn't a mistake'.

Snootlicker was buried under the lilac bush. It was his favorite place.

Daisy died six weeks after her friend was killed. She was buried beside him under the lilac bush. Lars said her time had come. She was old. Hilda added that it is possible to die of a broken heart. The following spring, when the lilacs were in bloom, the dark purple blossoms filled the air with their fragrance. The Johnsons stood there, and she took his big rough hand in hers and said, "They are together forever." It was the first time she had ever seen tears on her husband's face.

Scudder

Our daughter was twelve years old. We were between dogs, so to speak. She wanted a little poodle-type lap dog of any kind. My son and I did a lot of hunting so we wanted a hunting dog. It became a problem. Women use the word 'cute' to describe nearly everything. All baby animals are cute, but some can be more than that. How about darling, adorable, and even precious? My diabolical mind spoke to me. "Take Diana to a Labrador kennel."

Mayo Kellogg was a nationally known breeder and trainer of Labradors. He owned a large kennel near Madison, South Dakota. We were on our way to our cabin in Wisconsin, so this wasn't much out of the way. There were several pens of pups of all ages. Blacks and yellows. Chocolate Labs were very rare in those days. We spent an hour walking all around the place. Lots of cute babies. Diana is weakening. No hurry here. She asks, "Could I hold this one?" Bingo! We are soon on our way to the cabin with the kids and little Scudder in the car. Scudder was a very cute female yellow Lab.

When Scudder was only seven months old, we took her to Red Lake. On the way to the lake in early morning darkness, I spoke sagely to my 13-year-old son, Clay, "Don't expect much from Scudder. She is still a pup. It's her first experience and she might even be gun-shy. It will be good exercise for her and she will get better when she is older and has some training."

Red Lake is a huge shallow lake, more of a marsh. A duck paradise. At sunrise, a flock of redheads flew right in front of us. We dropped three. One was dead and two crippled. All three are within twenty feet of each other. Scudder swims out and quickly sizes up the situation. She ignores the dead duck, swims past the closest cripple on out to the furthest away. She grabs it in her mouth and starts back to us. She is nearly to us when the other cripple starts to swim away. She drops the live bird from her mouth and goes after the escaping duck. Nabs it and swims back towards us and the first cripple takes off again. She kept herding these two ducks in this manner until she retrieved both alive to us, and then went back for the dead one. Quite a first-time performance for a seven-month-old pup. My smart son grinned when he repeated my words of wisdom, "So she will get better when she has some training, huh, Dad?" Some dogs really don't need training. It is an innate thing. All they need is the opportunity. It does seem a shame and a waste to see a hunting dog living in a city without ever getting into the field to do what he would love to do. What he was born to enjoy.

We left Scudder with our friend, Mayne Talsma, when we took a short vacation. His ranch sprawled along the Missouri River. One day she was barking by his back porch. Barking excitedly. He went outside to check on her and saw that she had a huge rattlesnake cornered against the house. Mayne had killed some rattlesnakes before and took them to a neighbor's son who skinned and tanned them. The boy had complained that the skins were usually damaged. Mayne decided that this time he would deliver the perfect snake. He would take it alive. It wasn't easy. Scudder constantly jumped in and out of the snake's space. The buzzing was ominous. Mayne spotted his White Mountain ice cream freezer. The big outside part was nearby. A broom and a shovel leaned against the porch. An old window screen that he was going to repair someday was within reach. I would have loved to capture all this on film. Trying to keep his friend's dog from harm's way, using a shovel and a broom, picking up an angry rattlesnake, getting it into the ice cream freezer, and finally getting the screen over the top.

He drove into his neighbor's yard. When the lad saw what was in the back of the Jeep, his eyes widened. "I don't want to hear you complain about the condition of this one," Mayne admonished. There was a huge bulge in the snake's belly. It turned out to be a full-sized red fox squirrel.

In 1962, Rachel Carson wrote her bestseller, *Silent Spring*. It caused an increasing concern with ecology. She warned of the use of chemicals, herbicides, pesticides and damage to the environment. At that time, we still had as many as 70 finches at our feeders during the cold months of winter. Also, lots of blue jays, cardinals, and grosbeaks. Today, it is a rare privilege to see or even hear one of these birds in our yard.

In 1970, we still had a myriad of songbirds in our backyard. My dad, as a railroader, made wren houses that were perfect replicas of a train's caboose. The caboose was the last car on a freight train, having kitchen and sleeping facilities for the train crew. They were nearly always red. My dad traced around a quarter to determine the size of the hole he made to allow a wren to enter. This would keep all other birds out.

A pair of wrens checked out the caboose. We watched as they brought all sorts of stuff and poked it through the tiny hole. Wrens were our favorites. Busy, noisy, fearless. The female is nesting, while the male is singing his head off, "Look what I've done."

We checked the caboose every day. Finally, we heard the racket and chattering that announced the babies had left the nest. Both parents and three little ones were perched in the lower branches of our pear tree. Talk about nature's wonders. These two diminutive adults were feeding the three wee ones. They also took turns swooping down within inches of Scudder, who seemed to be minding her own business as she walked around in the yard. Then I noticed that something didn't look right. It appeared that Scudder had a mouthful of something. I called her to me. She sat in front of me as I asked, "What do you have in your mouth?" Really, did I expect her to answer?

I reached my hand down and held it under her nose. "Give me that. Give it to me. Spit it out." I finally resorted to, "Bad dog. You're a bad dog." Her ears drooped. Her jaws opened. Ptui. A baby wren tumbled into my hand. A very wet but unharmed petite thing. A piece of thread was tangled around its body. The thread must have been part of the nest, so the little bird couldn't fly like the other three and Scudder had caught it on the ground.

I took Scudder and the wren in the house to show Dorothy. We examined the baby and it appeared to be fine. Dorothy got a scissors and snipped the thread. I took the tiny bird back outside and placed it on the ground under the pear tree. When I retreated, I was chased and threatened by the parents.

The following morning, I was enjoying my coffee and newspaper on our screened-in front porch. I heard something hit the screen behind me. I turned and stared at four little wrens clinging to the outside. They stayed there long enough for Dorothy to come and see them, too. Their mother called them from the nearby willow tree. It was almost as if they had come to say goodbye. The next day, the entire family was gone.

When Scudder was twelve years old, we were at our cabin around October 1st. The fall colors of the Northwoods of Wisconsin rival those of New England. I took old Scudder back in those beautiful woods. If you knew the area, there were logging roads to follow. How quiet, peaceful. Before ATV's and snowmobiles. Deer, chickadees, nuthatches to enjoy. Once in awhile, as a special treat, the weird call of a loon drifted over a hill from an unseen lake nearby. As we returned and neared our cabin, I was close enough to smell the wood smoke wafting from the fireplace. Scudder was tired and walked slowly at my side. I am blind in my right eye, thanks that Jap hand grenade. So as luck would have it, a large blur charged down the hill from our right. A massive St. Bernard hit Scudder, knocked her down, and broke her hind leg. I took her to a vet. He gave me my options.

She is old; we love her. We can put her out of her misery or put a cast on the broken leg. I could see his point. It wasn't his dog. It was my decision to make. I opted for setting the bone and the cast. Bad choice. We left for South Dakota the next day. We stopped at pet areas at rest stops. I had to lift her in and out of the car. She couldn't squat to pee comfortably. The next day I took her to our local vet and had her mercifully put down.

When we take on a pet, we must realize that it won't live long, and ultimately it will cause us grief. Probably more often than not, we hate to play God and tend to keep these pets too long after they are visibly suffering. We allow our consciences and hearts to dictate what reality is calling for. We had a beagle named Duchess. She developed a kidney disorder. The vets prescribed various medications. Her hair fell out and she had a dandruff problem. Scratched constantly. Lost control of her bladder. I started to drive 20 miles to have her put away by the vet. Got 5 miles from home. She put her head on my lap and looked up at me as if to say, "I understand." I turned around and took her home. The next time I got 10 miles down the road. It took me three weeks and three trips before I finally did what I should have done the first time.

Sasha

We very carefully chose Sasha from a number of black and yellow pups at Mayo Kellogg's kennel. She was another yellow female and the youngest we ever had. This six-week-old puppy was placed in a small cardboard box that was put on the front seat of the car beside me. I stopped on side roads three times on our way home to put her in the grass of the ditch. I didn't want any accidents in the box. The most amazing thing about Sasha is that she never once had an accident in the house. She seemed to be born housebroken. Many dog owners have been skeptical of this and some just flat-out don't believe me. That first night, she slept in her box beside my bed. Twice she whined, woke me up and I took her outside. After a very short time, she slept all night.

When she was eight months old, she began to walk and run with a limp. The dreaded hip dysplasia was diagnosed. Kellogg offered to destroy her for us and said we could have another pup. Sasha was a classic Labrador beauty. Her coat was reddish gold. She was already part of the family.

We talked to our local vet. He had graduated from Iowa State University in Ames, Iowa. He informed us that they did hip replacements for dogs, and he would set up an appointment if we wanted to take her there. He also said it would be spendy—around $500 at that time. It would be much more today. I looked at Dorothy and immediately we nodded in agreement.

People in our small town couldn't believe we could spend that kind of money on a dog. I had comments like, "It's just a dumb dog." And, "Are you *nuts?*"

Our appointment was for 8:00 a.m., so we drove to Ames the day before. I found a small motel on the outskirts of town. A sleazy-looking bar was attached to the office. It had a big parking area for such a small motel. Ours was the only car visible in the entire place. The room was so small; the one bed was pushed against the wall. It was impossible to get in or out of the bed on that side. Dorothy admitted, "You do have a knack for finding luxurious motels."

I sensed sarcasm. "But isn't it nice and quiet? And we can keep Sasha in the room."

The sun went down. We heard activity in the parking area. Cars and motorcycles were arriving. The faint sound of a jukebox drifted from the bar at the other end of the motel. Then crash, boom-boom-boom—the music started in the parking lot. The dance had begun. Sasha crawled under the bed. The drums rattled the windows. It ended at 2:00 a.m. Activity also picked up in the motel. Doors in the hallway could be heard opening and closing. Some rooms were probably rented more than once that night.

The doctor and students called us at home to let us know that the surgery had gone well, and the patient was doing fine. Then, after a few more days, they called and said we could come and get her.

We entered a waiting room that looked exactly like we could have been in a hospital for people. They brought Sasha out on a leash. Her right hind leg had been shaved and it was held high in a sling. Several students crowded around to say goodbye and to give her farewell hugs. One said, "What a sweetheart. I wish all our patients had her disposition."

Sasha recovered and was in the field doing what she loved most. She wasn't 100% and she had a slight limp, but she could still chase and catch a crippled rooster. She probably had the best nose of all our dogs. Once our son, Clay, was driving along an old trail and spotted a covey of quail. He was alone and not hunting at the time, but he always had a shotgun with him. He stepped out of the rig and dropped three birds in heavy cover. He found one, but couldn't find the other two. He drove into town and got Sasha. They returned to the spot. Many dogs aren't interested in finding and retrieving birds if they haven't heard the gun or seen the birds fall. Clay let Sasha out, walked to the area and said, "Dead bird. Dead bird, Sasha." She found both quail.

The vets told us that Sasha would have some pain especially after a long day in the field. Half an aspirin or a baby aspirin would be fine. Keep in mind my Irish heritage. I enjoy a beer or a cocktail, especially manhattans. While some ethnic groups abhor drinking, I have seen German, Polish, Czech, Russian, and Italian communities embrace drinking as a way of life. Sort of a cakes and ale or all beer and skittles philosophy. Let the good times roll. C'est La Vie! The predominant ethnic group in our little area does not condone drinking. Then at the extreme end of the spectrum, the Mormons avoid spirits and even coffee and colas that contain caffeine. They might perhaps take an extra wife or two. To each his own.

It didn't take me long to discover that Sasha loved any alcoholic beverage. If I was working in the garden on a hot day and had a cold beer, I had to guard it or she would find and drink it. I didn't give it to her on purpose, but it is a pain killer and more fun than aspirin.

We had a fun backyard cookout with about 20 people. Brats, burgers, potato salad, baked beans, cocktails and beer. The whole nine yards. Sasha enjoyed the people and the special attention she received. What a nice, sweet, loving dog. She moved around from person to person while ignoring the food. However, she stalked her victims and waited for them to set a drink on the ground or on a low tray. This was an Irish Labrador. We should have named her Kathleen or Maggie. One young lady, sitting in a lawn chair, had her martini on the ground beside her. She caught Sasha slurping her Beefeaters. This Irish lass, name of Carmody, grabbed the glass and scolded, "Say that's mine!" And proceeded to drink it anyway. How many women would do that? My kind of woman.

My favorite vehicle was a 1967 GMC Jimmy. A 4x4 that had a head-bolt heater for starting in the winter. Never plugged it in. It started every morning even in sub-zero weather. It was my hunting and fishing rig. Each morning and evening, no matter what kind of weather, I took Sasha out for a run in the country. It was good for her, and I rarely had to clean her pen. More than one person told me that if they believed in reincarnation, they would like to come back as one of my dogs.

Maybe two or three times each year, we drive, early in the morning, forty miles to an Indian casino to have breakfast and make a donation to the Tribe. More often than not, we don't meet another vehicle in the entire forty miles. This is a nice blacktop road that follows the Missouri River. We see pheasants, turkeys, deer, and eagles along the way. I hope I won't be considered an out-and-out menace or criminal as I relate what Paul Harvey would call "The Rest of the Story".

There is a desolate un-maintained dirt road near town. After a big rain, it is so muddy no one attempts it. It might also be impossible due to snowdrifts in the winter. This was one of my favorite roads to take Sasha. Sometimes I walked with her, but usually I drove very slowly while she worked the ditches on both sides of the road. We live in a State Prison town. There are as many inmates in the prison as there are residents of the town. During our daily evening ritual in the country, I looked forward to relaxing and taking a big ice-filled manhattan to sip.

Over a period of years, I could count the number of people on one hand that I had seen on this road. I am sipping my manhattan as I watch Sasha inhaling scent. How does she weed out the smells of meadowlarks or crows and still concentrate on game birds? I am nearly mesmerized as I watch this dog. I glance at the road ahead and see a highway patrol car approaching. I open the door, call Sasha, and she grudgingly jumps in and over the seat into the back. I reach down and push my drink under the seat. As he came closer, the patrolman held his arm out the window and signaled me to stop. "Hi, Wayne, I see you have your dog out for its exercise. Good looking dog."

We are side-by-side, close enough to reach out and shake hands. "What's going on?" I ask.

At this point, Sasha jumps from the back into the empty front seat and then down on the floor with her head under my seat. This is not good.

The officer says, "We've got a runner, but he won't get far. It sure will help when they get all that razor wire up on the fence around the prison."

Slurp, slurp, slurp. "Yeah, that stuff isn't pretty, but it must do the job."

Slurp, slurp.

"Take care, Wayne." He drives slowly away.

Sasha jumps onto the front seat and then dutifully into the back.

I reached under the seat and retrieved my empty glass. She even ate the cherry. No sign of remorse or guilt. It was better than aspirin.

As Sasha grew old we acquired two more dogs. A yellow female Lab and a female Chesapeake. Brandy and Sadie. I frequently took all three dogs hunting partly because I couldn't stand to leave one in the pen. Besides, it was triple the pleasure to watch three working together. I nearly always hunted alone and never with more than one other person.

On one of these days, I was hunting around a bunch of old farm buildings. The cover was heavy. A pheasant erupted. Its shrill cackle made my heart beat faster. I pulled the trigger as it sailed over a dilapidated shed. A poor shot resulted in a crippled bird. We walked around the shed to find a big patch of weeds taller than my head. The dogs plunged in this thick stuff while I waited on the outside. At this moment, a new 4-wheel-drive vehicle drove in the yard. I could spot an out-of-state license plate.

Three hunters got out and walked over to me.

"Do you have permission to hunt here?"

"Yes, I do. I've hunted here for years."

"I was just curious, because the owner is a friend of mine, and he usually doesn't allow hunting on his property."

Sadie came out of the weed patch and plunged back in. "Nice looking Chesapeake."

Brandy appeared briefly and disappeared.

"You've got two dogs?" the same man asked.

Now Sasha comes out of the heavy stuff, nose to the ground, and goes to a corncrib. There is a big badger hole by the side of the crib. She puts her head in the hole, then her front shoulders, then digs the passage a bit bigger.

"Looks like you've got a badger dog. You had better hope the badger isn't home." They all chuckle. "Are you sure you have enough dogs?" More laughter.

Sasha is farther down the hole with only her hind legs and tail visible. She begins to back out while painfully wiggling and maneuvering. When she finally frees herself, she has the live pheasant in her mouth. She brings it to me and then vigorously shakes dirt all over everyone.

For the first time, one of the other hunters spoke. "I don't believe what I just saw."

The third hunter chimed in. "You really don't need three dogs, do you? We don't have a dog. Would you sell us this one?"

"Sorry, she's not for sale."

"How about one of those others?"

"None of my dogs are for sale."

The first guy who had done most of the talking asked, "Aren't you even going to ask how much we would be willing to pay?"

"No."

The three of them exchanged glances and were silent. The vocal one said, "Too bad we didn't have a dog about an hour ago. We dropped a pheasant deader than hell. It just crumpled. Feathers flew all over, and it fell stone dead in some heavy stuff. Not as thick as this, though. We looked for a long time and never did find it."

"Where was this?"

They described where they had been. "I know where that is. I'd be happy to take the dogs there, and maybe they can find it. I can't promise anything." It has been over an hour, and they didn't see the bird go down. "I'll meet you in a few minutes."

I gave the dogs a drink of water. I can't remember where the guys were from...Arkansas, Oklahoma, Texas?

They were waiting for me. A small tree stood in the middle of a slough. There were weeds and cattails, but they all agreed that the dead rooster fell at the base of the tree. This helped a lot. We walked to the tree, and I tried to work up some excitement and enthusiasm in the dogs. I said excitedly, "Dead bird in here. Hunt 'em up in here. Dead bird."

It worked. They combed the place thoroughly. Then Brandy sneaked out into the open and headed north. One of the guys exclaimed, "Your dog is running away. What's its name?"

"Brandy."

He yelled, "Brandy, come back here, Brandy." He put his fingers in his mouth and whistled. She disappeared over a hill about a hundred yards away. The other two dogs had become lethargic. Their hearts weren't in this game.

After searching a few more minutes, one of the guys said, "We had better be going. It's getting late. I hope your dog comes back." They headed toward their rig.

I looked to the north just as Brandy popped over the ridge. "I could tell by her gait and the way she held her head high, she was carrying something.

"I called to the hunters, "I think I see your pheasant coming."

Brandy held the pheasant by the back. Its head was up and its legs were still churning as if trying to run. She proudly brought it to me. I asked which guy had shot it. When he raised his hand, I handed it to him and said, "Here is your dead bird."

The guy grinned and said, "This was worth the trip up here. I can't thank you enough."

We walked to our vehicles. I reached inside the Jimmy and picked up Sasha's pheasant. "Here, take this one, too." They feebly protested.

"No problem," I insisted, "I have lots of pheasants in our freezer. This is a one-shot deal for you. I hunt every day."

"You are a lucky man."

"I know."

All three guys had to say goodbye to each dog. They spoke to them by name and patted each on the head and rubbed their flanks. I was proud of my girls.

Sadie

Our Chesapeake had a luxurious reddish-brown coat. It was so thick it felt something like steel wool when you stroked her back. Her personality was unlike the Labradors. She was rather standoffish and wary of strangers, but she was very affectionate and loyal to the family. She was a dainty eater and bordered on being finicky. She was always the last to finish eating. The other dogs never tried to steal her food, because she was bigger and stronger. The pecking order rule. Labradors are easy to please. They will eat anything and everything. Just put the food in front of them and step back. They don't eat. They inhale the food. They are voracious. I'm not sure they have taste buds. Let's face it: Labradors are regular garbage guts.

Sadie enjoyed hunting upland game birds, but they weren't her passion. She went along for the fellowship, exercise, and to escape the pen. She didn't have the keen nose of the Labs, but she watched them when they got excited, and she hunted more by sight than by scent. Once in awhile, though, she would stumble on a downed pheasant, quail, or grouse before the Labs found it.

She had such a soft mouth; she could have carried an egg in it. She also had, however, one bad habit in the field. Every time I took her dove hunting, she couldn't resist eating the first bird that was shot. Only the first bird. I always hated to see owners beat their dogs. The second time she ate a dove, I whacked her a couple of times and scolded her. That should take care of that. It didn't. She must have been a gourmet of fine food. Even though she knew she was doing something wrong, she just could not and would not pass up that first succulent little bird. About three chomps and one gulp. Almost pitiful. She would practically crawl to me with feathers in the corner of her mouth and tail down between her legs. The expression in her face said it all. "Don't hit me. Please forgive me. I can't help myself."

Duck hunting was a different story. This was Sadie's forte. She was an awesome powerful swimmer. The Labs were good, but she was better. We hunted the backwaters of the Missouri River. Sixty decoys complemented our blind. Once in awhile, Sadie would become entangled in a decoy string while retrieving a duck. It was a bit scary, but she would simply do her job and end up on shore with the duck and the decoy with anchor attached.

Sadie would sit in the blind for hours. She never took her eyes off the skies. My friends knew of my vision problems, but they were amazed at how I could spot incoming ducks before they ever saw them. Some things are best kept secret. I felt almost smug. Truthfully, I watched Sadie. She was like radar. When her ears pricked forward and her eyes widened, I simply watched where she was looking. Then I would whisper to my friends in the blind, "Get ready," and I would nod in the direction that Sadie was looking. She could spot ducks before they were tiny specks on the horizon. Truthfully, I was the last to see the ducks come in. Sometimes they were almost over the decoys. I used to wonder what went through Sadie's mind. I suspect that she might have already identified the species before we saw them. She might have been saying to herself. "Here comes a flock of woodies. I hope these guys don't blow it."

The storytelling, hot coffee, and food are part of the duck blind. Old Sadie provided 90% of the pleasure of duck hunting over decoys. I wonder if they hunt ducks in dog heaven?

Brandy

It has been said that when young Fred Astaire had his Hollywood screen test, someone viewed the film, put it in a can and wrote on the lid:

Astaire, Fred
Can't act.
Can't sing.
Dances a little.

The American Kennel Club judges, trainers, and handlers are always looking for prototype Labradors. Big, long legs, rugged.

Just a glance at little Brandy and these experts would have agreed:
Brandy
Runt of the litter.
Too short.
Could make a nice pet.
Might hunt a little.
A sparrow among the robins and bluebirds.

A big heart more than compensated for Brandy's lack of stature. She was, by far, the most zealous of all our hunting dogs. As an old coach, I have often described athletes as being fast or quick. She was both. She never stopped hunting. It was amazing to see her working cover over her head. At times she would leap into the air like she was on a pogo stick or a trampoline. Her stamina was unbelievable. Between fields, other dogs would lie down, pant, and rest in the back of the Bronco, Jimmy, or pickup. She wanted in the front seat to watch out the windshield to check out the ditches and fields while road hunting. In the pen, all year round, she was constantly watching for squirrels and rabbits that she considered intruders in her yard. At night, after a long day in the field, the other dogs would sleep soundly and snored loudly. At the same time, Brandy would be dreaming and still hunting in her sleep with legs moving while emitting little whines and yips.

Clay was hunting Sasha, Sadie, and Brandy when they jumped a coyote out of a ravine. They chased it out of sight and then returned. Our dogs always chase coyotes and deer for a short distance. What was their purpose? Of course, they never caught one. I don't think they expected to catch one. Was it in their job description? Sort of a fun divergence?

Clay walked along a ridge with plum thickets, too thick to walk in, below. A brilliant cock pheasant had sneaked ahead and protested as he exploded into the air. It was a long shot, but you can chance that when you are hunting three dogs. The crippled pheasant wobbled in the air and finally sailed into a small tree in a fence line. This was visible to all three dogs. It was also obvious that this pheasant had chosen his last and best survival. Naturally, the dogs beat Clay to the site. The bird alighted in this small tree about nine feet off the ground. The dogs were circling their quarry.

Brandy sized up the situation. This was sort of a bush-like tree with thick branches that came nearly to the ground. The pheasant was clinging to a branch about four feet from the trunk. Brandy began climbing up through the thick plentiful branches. She reached the limb claimed by the pheasant then lost her footing and came tumbling down through the foliage. She hit the ground with a thump. This tenacious little dog immediately attacked the tree again. This time more boldly. She knew she could do it, so she quickly reached the prized limb. She tested it gingerly. She was eyeball to eyeball with her pheasant. Only a few more inches. She reached for it, missed, and both came crashing down through the branches. Now there are three very eager dogs and one pheasant. During the ensuing melee, Clay snatched the bird from the ground to avoid competition. He patted each dog on the head as he praised, "Good dogs. Fine dogs. Are we having fun?"

Applause came from the nearby road. Two Minnesota hunters were leaning against their station wagon. They had witnessed the entire performance. Clay walked over to visit with them. They were smiling and shaking their heads. "We can't believe what we just saw. A dog that climbs trees? Our friends in Minneapolis won't believe it, either."

"She is pretty special. I never know what to expect from her next," Clay admitted.

"We sure would like to buy that little dog. How much would you take for it?"

"I won't sell her."

"Come on. Shoot us a price."

"No sale."

"We understand. Think how much better that little dog will get when it grows up."

"She isn't going to grow up."

"Are you kidding? Why not?"

"Because she is four years old. She was the runt of the litter, and no one wanted her. We lucked out."

What an understatement.

Many men that I know are blessed with the skills needed to do 'handy' things around the house. Wives admire men like this. I'm talking about plumbing, electrical work, carpentry. Name it. These same guys can spend hours browsing in hardware stores, Home Depot, and Menards. My 'do-it-yourself' ranking, on a scale of 1 to 10, would probably be a negative 8. I have a problem putting new batteries in a flashlight.

So, when we need things done at our cabin in Wisconsin, I'm helpless. Thankfully, we have known a wonderful young man who has lived nearby since he was in high school. He is in his forties now and for years has put our dock in the water in the spring, primes and starts the pump on the well, shovels the deep snow off the roof in winter, and reverses all this by closing up in late fall. So dependable and almost like family. Rick is very personable, and we always enjoy visiting with him when he stops by to fill us in on fishing reports and news from around the lake.

He recently came to the cabin to get paid for some work he had done. After the usual banter and conversation, Rick surprised me with a sudden shocking announcement. "A couple of weeks ago, my wife and I were having breakfast, and out of left field she goes, 'I want a divorce.'"

"Why?"

"I'm not happy."

"Hey, let's get some counseling."

"I don't need counseling. I don't want counseling. I want a divorce. I'm not happy."

Rick smiled wryly. "You know, Wayne, that's the first time I've ever lost my appetite for pancakes and sausage." Silence, as he stared wistfully through the window at the lake. He resumed:

"If you're not happy, I won't stand in your way. I certainly don't want to live with someone who doesn't want to be with me. Can we still be friends?"

"Yes."

"Maybe go to dinner sometime?"

"Maybe."

"We will have to get a lawyer."

"I've already done that."

"Could we use the same lawyer? It would save money."

"Why not?"

I asked, "How long were you married?"

"Twenty-four years. The lawyer told me this should be a real piece of cake. Both parties agree. No real animosity. Many divorces become vicious and bitter. Very little money involved and above all, no children. The waiting period will probably be shortened. How lucky can I get?" Again that wistful smile.

I waited for him to regain his composure. Then the dam broke and he blurted, "Do you remember my little dog, Peanuts?"

"Of course I do. He was like your shadow. I never saw you without him beside you in your pickup. "I noticed he wasn't with you today."

"He died two days after my wife moved out. He was fourteen years old. That little mutt died just when I needed him most. He was my buddy." Tears down both cheeks. "That wasn't the best week of my life."

"This too shall pass, Rick. Hang in there," I offered lamely. I gave him a hug and he started to leave. He opened the door and paused for a moment. I barely heard him softly murmur, "Ya know, I already miss my dog more than I miss my wife."